The Gnostic Gospel of Thomas: Wholeness, Enlightenment, and Individuation

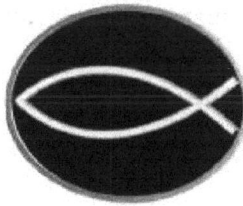

Joseph B. Lumpkin

The Gnostic Gospel of Thomas:
Wholeness, Enlightenment, and Individuation

For information about first time authors, contact Fifth Estate
2795 County Hwy 57, Blountsville, AL 35031.

First Edition
Cover art by An Quigley
Printed on acid-free paper

Library of Congress Control No: 2012939349

ISBN: 9781936533275

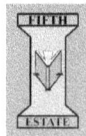

Fifth Estate, 2012

Dedication

To fellow travelers;

When we have become detached we can see clearly;

When we become whole, uniting mind, emotion, and spirit we are saved.

Jesus said: Become passers-by.

Jesus said: If you bring forth what is within you, it will save you. If you do not have it within you to bring forth, that which you lack will destroy you.

Table of Contents

Introduction and History

In the winter of 1945, in Upper Egypt, an Arab peasant was gathering fertilizer and topsoil for his crops. While digging in the soft dirt he came across a large earthen vessel. Inside were scrolls containing hitherto unseen books.

The scrolls were discovered near the site of the ancient town of Chenoboskion, at the base of a mountain named Gebel et-Tarif, near Hamra-Dum, in the vicinity of Naj 'Hammadi, about sixty miles from Luxor in Egypt. The texts were written in the Coptic language and preserved on papyrus sheets. The lettering style dated them as having been penned around the third or fourth century A.D. The Gospel of Thomas is the longest of the volumes consisting of 114 verses. Recent study indicates that the original work of Thomas, of which the scrolls are copies, may predate the four canonical gospels of Matthew, Mark, Luke, and John. The origin of The Gospel of Thomas is now thought to be from the first or second century A.D.

The word Coptic is an Arabic corruption of the Greek word Aigyptos, which in turn comes from the word Hikaptah, one of the names of the city of Memphis, the first capital of ancient Egypt.

There has never been a Coptic state or government per se, however the word has been used to generally define a culture and language present in the area of Egypt.

The known history of the Copts starts with King Mina the first King, who united the northern and southern kingdoms of Egypt circa 3050 B.C. The ancient Egyptian civilization under the rule of the Pharaohs lasted over 3000 years. Saint Mina (named after the king) is one of the major Coptic saints. He was martyred in 309 A.D.

The culture has come to be recognized as one containing a distinctive art, architecture, and even a certain Christian church system.

The Coptic Church is based on the teachings of St. Mark, who introduced the region to Christianity in the first century A.D. The Copts take pride in the monastic flavor of their church and the fact that the Gospel of Mark is thought to be the oldest of the Gospels. Now, lying before a peasant boy was a scroll written in the ancient Coptic tongue; The Gospel of Thomas, possibly older than and certainly quite different from any other Gospel.

The peasant boy who found the treasure of the Gospel of Thomas stood to be rewarded greatly. This could have been the discovery of a lifetime for his family, but the boy had no idea what he had. He took the scrolls home, where his mother burned some as kindling. Others were sold to the black market antique dealers in Cairo. It would be years until they found their way into the hands of a scholar.

Part of the thirteenth codex was smuggled from Egypt to America. In 1955 whispers of the existence of the codex had reached the ears of Gilles Quispel, a professor of religion and history in the Netherlands. The race was on to find and translate the scrolls.

The introduction of the collected sayings of Jesus refers to the writer as Didymus (Jude) Thomas. This is the same Thomas who doubted Jesus and was then told to place his hand within the breach in the side of the Savior. In the Gospel of St. John, he is referred to as Didymus, which means twin in Greek. In Aramaic, the name Jude (or Judas) also carries the sense of twin. The use of this title led some in the apocryphal tradition to believe that he was the twin brother and confidant of Jesus. However, when applied to Jesus himself, the literal meaning of twin must be rejected by orthodox Christianity as well as anyone adhering to the doctrine of the virgin birth of the only begotten Son of God. The title is likely meant to signify that Thomas was a close confidant of Jesus, or more simply, he was part of a set of twins and in no way related to Jesus.

Ancient church historians mention that Thomas preached to the Parthians in Persia and it is said he was buried in Edessa. Fourth century chronicles attribute the evangelization of India (Asia-Minor or Central Asia) to Thomas.

The text, which some believe predates the four gospels, has a very Taoist, Zen-like, or Eastern flavor. Since it is widely held that the four gospels of Matthew, Mark, Luke, and John have a common reference in the basic text of Mark, it stands to reason that all follow the same general history, insights, and language. Since scholars believe that the Gospel of Thomas predates the four main gospels, it can be assumed it was written outside the influences common to the other gospels.

The Gospel of Thomas is actually not a gospel at all. It contains no narrative but is instead a collection of sayings, which are said to be from Jesus himself as written (quoted) by Thomas. Although the codex found in Egypt is dated to the fourth century, most biblical scholars place the actual construction of the text of Thomas at about 40 – 150 A.D.

The gospel was often mentioned in early Christian literature, but no copy was thought to have survived until the discovery of the Coptic manuscript. Since then, part of the Oxyrynchus papyri have been identified as older Greek fragments of Thomas. The papyri were discovered in 1898 in the rubbish heaps of Oxyrhynchus, Egypt. This discovery yielded over thirty-five manuscript fragments for the New Testament. They have been dated to about 60 A.D. As a point of reference, a fragment of papyrus from the Dead Sea Scrolls had been dated to before 68 A.D.

There are marked differences between the Greek and Coptic texts, as we will see.

The debate on the date of Thomas centers in part on whether Thomas is dependent upon the canonical gospels, or is derived from an earlier document that was simply a collection of sayings. Many of the passages in Thomas appear to be more authentic versions of the synoptic parables, and many have parallels in Mark and Luke. This has caused a division of thought wherein some believe Thomas used common sources also used by Mark and Luke. Others believe Thomas was written independently after witnessing the same events.

If Thomas wrote his gospel first, without input from Mark, and from the standpoint of Eastern exposure as a result of his sojourn into India, it could explain the mystical quality of the text. It could also explain the striking differences in the recorded quotes of Jesus as memories were influenced by exposure to Asian culture.

There is some speculation that the sayings found in Thomas could be more accurate to the original intent and wording of Jesus than the other gospels. This may seem counter-intuitive until we realize that Christianity itself is an Eastern religion, albeit Middle-Eastern. Although, as it spread west the faith went through many changes to westernize or Romanize it...Jesus was both mystical and Middle-Eastern. The Gospel of Thomas may not have seen as much "dilution" by Western society.

The Gospel of Thomas is so old that it is seen as evidence of the Q or Quelle Source document. The Q document is thought to be a written document predating the gospels and used as a common source for the gospels. It was thought to more heavily influence the gospels of Matthew and Luke. Now, this source is seen in a more pure and uncorrupted form in Thomas.

Marilyn Mellowes, writing for "Frontline," reports: "In 1989, a team of researchers led by James M. Robinson of the Institute for Antiquity and Christianity in Claremont, CA, began a most unlikely task: the "reconstruction" of the Gospel of Q. Robinson and his team are accomplishing this by a highly detailed literary analysis of Matthew, Luke, and Thomas. Their painstaking work goes "verse by verse, word by word, case ending by case ending."

The "recovery" of the Q gospel has stimulated a debate about the nature of early Christian communities, and by extension, the origins of Christianity itself. One scholar, Burton Mack, has advanced a radical thesis: that at least some Christian communities did not see Jesus as a Messiah; they saw him as a teacher of wisdom, a man who tried to teach others how to live. For them, Jesus was not divine, but fully human. These first followers of Jesus differed from other Christians whose ritual and practice was centered on the death and the resurrection of Jesus. They did not emerge as the "winners" of history; perhaps because maintaining the faith required the existence of a story that included not only the life of Jesus but also his Passion."

For more information of the beliefs of Christians in the first 50 years of the faith please see, "The Didache: A Different Faith, A Different Salvation" published by Fifth Estate Publishing.

The Gospel of Thomas was most likely composed in Syria, where tradition holds the church of Edessa was founded by Judas Thomas, The Twin (Didymos). The gospel may well be the earliest written tradition in the Syriac church

The Gospel of Thomas is sometimes called a Gnostic Gospel, although it seems more likely Thomas was adopted by the Gnostic community and interpreted in the light of their beliefs.

The term Gnostic is derived from gnosis, which in Greek means knowledge. Gnostics believed that knowledge is formed or found from a personal encounter with God brought about by inward or intuitive insight. It is this knowledge that brings salvation. The Gnostics believed they were privy to a secret knowledge about the divine. It is their focus on knowledge that leads to their name. The roots of the Gnosticism pre-date Christianity. Similarities exist between Gnosticism and the wisdom and knowledge cults found in Egypt. The belief system seems to have spread and found a suitable home in the mystical side of the Christian faith.

There are numerous references to the Gnostics in second century literature. Their form of Christianity was considered heresy by the early church fathers. The intense resistance to the Gnostic belief system seems to be based in two areas. First, there was a general Gnostic belief that we were all gods, with heaven contained within us. Jesus, according to the Gnostics, was here to show us our potential to become as he was; a son or daughter of god, for God is both father and mother, male and female. These beliefs ran contrary to the newly developing orthodoxy. The second line of resistance was political. This resistance developed later and would have come from the fact that a faith based on a personal encounter flew in the face of the developing church political structure that placed priests and church as the keepers of heaven's gate with salvation through them alone.

It is from the writings condemning the group that we glean most of our information about the Gnostics. They are alluded to in the Bible in 1 Tm. 1:4 and 1 Tm. 6:20, and possibly the entirety of Jude, as the writers of the Bible defended their theology against that of the Gnostics.

Keeping in mind that the winners write the history, we see only what the emerging orthodoxy wishes us to see of the alleged evils of Gnosticism. Men of the orthodoxy were howling about Gnostics claiming that heaven was within each of us, viewing this as heresy, seeing that heaven could not possibly be there since the church controlled our entrance to heaven.

The main point regarding Gnostics is that they seek knowledge, which is not "informational" but instead is of a "revelatory" nature, noting the fact that Jesus taught not so much in factual information but instead spoke in ways calculated to awaken a deeper knowledge within the person, thus giving them a type of transcendental knowledge possible only through spiritual resurrection as if one were to remember the origin of the soul and what was there.

Beyond this central point of belief there existed several types or denominations of Gnostics, varying from those who seemed to clog this simple doctrine with myths and cosmologies of unimagined complexities, to those who were seeking a change of spiritual state, as opposed to simply changing belief systems from one religion to the next. For information beyond this simple point we should have a quick lesson in the history and general scope of beliefs within various Gnostic communities.

What is Gnosticism?

"Gnosticism: A system of religion mixed with Greek and Oriental philosophy of the 1st through 6th centuries A.D. Intermediate between Christianity and paganism, Gnosticism taught that knowledge rather than faith was the greatest good and that through knowledge alone could salvation be attained."

Webster's Dictionary

The word Gnostic is based on the Greek word "Gnosis," which means "knowledge." The "Gnosis" is the knowledge of the ultimate, supreme God and his spirit, which is contained within us all. It is this knowledge that allows one to transcend this material world with its falsities and spiritual entrapments and ascend into heaven to be one with God.

For centuries the definition of Gnosticism has in itself been a point of confusion and contention within the religious community. This is due in part to the ever-broadening application of the term and the fact that various sects of Gnosticism existed as the theology evolved and began to merge into what became mainstream Christianity.

Even though Gnosticism continued to evolve, it is the theology in place at the time that the Gnostic Gospels were written that should be considered and understood before attempting to render or read a translation. To do otherwise would make the translation cloudy and obtuse.

It becomes the duty of both translator and reader to understand the ideas being espoused and the terms conveying those ideas. A grasp of theology, cosmology, and relevant terms is necessary for a clear transmission of the meaning within the text in question.

With this in mind, we will briefly examine Gnostic theology, cosmology, and history. We will focus primarily on Gnostic sects existing in the first through fourth centuries A.D. since it is believed most Gnostic Gospels were written during that time. It was also during that time that reactions within the emerging Christian orthodoxy began to intensify.

The downfall of many books written on the topic of religion is the attempt to somehow remove history and people from the equation. History shapes religion because it shapes the perception and direction of religious leaders. Religion also develops and evolves in an attempt to make sense of the universe as it is seen and understood at the time. Thus, to truly grasp a religious concept it is important to know the history, people, and cosmology of the time. These areas are not separate but are continually interacting.

A Brief Lesson
In Gnosticism

The roots of Gnosticism may pre-date Christianity. Similarities exist between Gnosticism and the wisdom and mystery cults found in Egypt and Greece. Gnosticism contains the basic terms and motifs of Plato's cosmology as well as the mystical qualities of Buddhism. Plato was steeped in Greek mythology, and the Gnostic creation myth has elements owing to this. Both cosmology and mysticism within Gnosticism present an interpretation of Christ's existence and teachings, thus, Gnostics are considered to be a Christian sect. Gnostic followers are urged to look within themselves for the truth and the Christ spirit hidden, asleep in their souls. The battle cry can be summed up in the words of the Gnostic Gospel of Thomas, verse 3:

Jesus said: If those who lead you say to you: Look, the Kingdom is in the sky, then the birds of the sky would enter before you. If they say to you: It is in the sea, then the fish of the sea would enter ahead of you. But the Kingdom of God exists within you and it exists outside of you. Those who come to know (recognize) themselves will find it, and when you come to know yourselves you will become known and you will realize that you are the children of the Living Father. Yet if you do not come to know yourselves then you will dwell in poverty and it will be you who are that poverty.

Paganism was a religious traditional society in the Mediterranean leading up to the time of the Gnostics. Centuries after the conversion of Constantine, mystery cults worshipping various Egyptian and Greco-Roman gods continued. These cults taught that through their secret knowledge worshippers could control or escape the mortal realm. The Gnostic doctrine of inner knowledge and freedom may have part of its roots here. The concept of duality and inner guidance taught in Buddhism added to and enforced Gnostic beliefs, as we will see later.

The belief systems of Plato, Buddha, and paganism melted together, spread, and found a suitable home in the mystical side of the Christian faith as it sought to adapt and adopt certain Judeo-Christian beliefs and symbols.

Like modern Christianity, Gnosticism had various points of view that could be likened to Christian denominations of today. Complex and elaborate creation myths took root in Gnosticism, being derived from those of Plato. Later, the theology evolved and Gnosticism began to shed some of its more unorthodox myths, leaving the central theme of inner knowledge or gnosis to propagate.

The existence of various sects of Gnosticism, differing creation stories, along with the lack of historical documentation, has left scholars in a quandary about exactly what Gnostics believed. Some have suggested that the Gnostics represented a free thinking and idealistic movement much like that of the "Hippie" movement active in the United States during the 1960's.

Just as the "Hippie" movement in the U.S. influenced political thought, some early sects of Gnostics began to exert direct influence on the Christian church and its leadership.

Although it appears that there were several sects of Gnosticism, we will attempt to discuss the more universal Gnostic beliefs along with the highlights of the major sects.

Gnostic cosmology, (which is the theory of how the universe is created, constructed, and sustained), is complex and very different from orthodox Christianity cosmology. In many ways Gnosticism may appear to be polytheistic or even pantheistic.

To understand some of the basic beliefs of Gnosticism, let us start with the common ground shared between Gnosticism and modern Christianity. Both believe the world is imperfect, corrupt, and brutal. The blame for this, according to mainstream Christianity, is placed squarely on the shoulders of man himself. With the fall of man (Adam), the world was forever changed to the undesirable and harmful place in which we live today. However, Gnostics reject this view as an incorrect interpretation of the creation myth.

According to Gnostics, the blame is not in ourselves, but in our creator. The creator of this world was himself somewhat less than perfect and in fact, deeply flawed and cruel, making mankind the child of a lesser God. It is in the book, *The Apocryphon of John*, that the Gnostic view of creation is presented to us in great detail.

Gnosticism also teaches that in the beginning a Supreme Being called The Father, The Divine All, The Origin, The Supreme God, or The Fullness, emanated the element of existence, both visible and invisible. His intent was not to create but, just as light emanates from a flame, so did creation shine forth from God. This manifested the primal element needed for creation. This was the creation of Barbelo, who is the Thought of God.

Barbelo is the perfect mother, brought into existence by the perfect and whole God.

The Father's thought performed a deed and she was created from it. It is she who had appeared before him in the shining of his light. This is the first power which was before all of them and which was created from his mind. She is the Thought of the All and her light shines like his light. It is the perfect power which is the visage of the invisible. She is the pure, undefiled Spirit who is perfect. She is the first power, the glory of Barbelo, the perfect glory of the kingdom (kingdoms), the glory revealed. She glorified the pure, undefiled Spirit and it was she who praised him, because thanks to him she had come forth.
The Apocryphon of John

It could be said that Barbelo is the creative emanation and, like the Divine All, is both male and female. It is the "agreement" of Barbelo and the Divine All, representing the union of male and female, that created the Christ Spirit and all the Aeons. In some renderings the word "Aeon" is used to designate an ethereal realm or kingdom. In other versions "Aeon" indicates the ruler of the realm. One of these rulers was called Sophia or Wisdom. Her fall began a chain of events that led to the introduction of evil into the universe.

Seeing the Divine flame of God, Sophia sought to know its origin. She sought to know the very nature of God. Sophia's passion ended in tragedy when she managed to capture a divine and creative spark, which she attempted to duplicate with her own creative force, without the union of a male counterpart. She attempted to bring forth something from herself as God had brought Barbelo from his own perfection, but Sophia was not perfect and she was not God. It was this act of overreaching by Sophia that produced the Archons, beings born outside the higher divine realm. In the development of the myth, explanations seem to point to the fact that Sophia carried the divine essence of creation from God within her but chose to attempt creation by using her own powers. It is unclear if this was in an attempt to understand the Supreme God and his power, or an impetuous act that caused evil to enter the cosmos in the form of her creations.

The realm containing the Fullness of the Godhead and Sophia is called the pleroma or Realm of Fullness. This is the Gnostic heaven. The lesser Gods created in Sophia's failed attempt were cast outside the pleroma and away from the presence of God. In essence, she threw away and discarded her flawed creations, who had a lion's head and a serpent's body.

"She cast it away from her, outside the place where no one of the immortals might see it, for she had created it in ignorance. And she surrounded it with a glowing cloud, and she put a throne in the middle of the cloud so that no one could see it except the Holy Spirit who is called the mother of all that has life. And she called his name Yaldabaoth." Apocryphon of John

The beings Sophia created were imperfect and oblivious to the Supreme God. Her creations contained deities even less perfect than herself. They were called the Powers, the Rulers, or the Archons. These evil, spiteful, jealous creatures are the ones referred to by St. Paul when he stated that our fight is against "principalities, powers, and rulers of darkness in high places." Their leader was called the Demiurge, but his name was Yaldabaoth. It was the flawed, imperfect, spiritually blind Demiurge, (Yaldabaoth), who became the creator of the material world and all things in it. Demiurge means, "the half-maker." Gnostics considered Yaldabaoth to be the same as Jehovah (Yahweh), who is the Jewish creator God. These beings, the Demiurge and the Archons, would later equate to Satan and his demons, or Jehovah and his angels, depending on which Gnostic sect is telling the story.

The making of the world is ascribed to a company of seven Archons (a type of deity somewhat equated to an angel). Their chief is "Yaldabaoth" (also known as "Yaltabaoth" or "Ialdabaoth").

The Apocryphon of John, written around 120 A.D. recounts that the Demiurge arrogantly declares that he has made the world by himself:

Now the archon (ruler) who is weak has three names. The first name is Yaltabaoth, the second is Saklas ("fool"), and the third is Samael (god of the blind or blind god). And he is impious in his arrogance which is in him. For he said, "I am God and there is no other God beside me," for he is ignorant of his strength, the place from which he had come.

He is Demiurge and maker of man, but as a ray of light from above enters the body of man and gives him a soul, Yaldabaoth is filled with envy; he tries to limit man's knowledge by forbidding him the fruit of knowledge in paradise. The Demiurge, fearing lest Jesus, whom he had intended as his Messiah, should spread the knowledge of the Supreme God, had him crucified by the Romans. At the consummation of all things all light will return to the Pleroma. But Yaldabaoth, the Demiurge, with the material world, will be cast into the lower depths.

In the Gnostic text, Pistis Sophia, Yaldabaoth has already sunk from his high estate and resides in Chaos, where, with his forty-nine demons, he tortures wicked souls in boiling rivers of pitch, and with other punishments (pp. 257, 382).

Yaldabaoth is frequently called "the Lion-faced", leontoeides, with the body of a serpent. We are told also, that the Demiurge is of a fiery nature, the words of Moses being applied to him, "the Lord our God is a burning and consuming fire," a text used also by Simon. He is an archon with the face of a lion, half flame and half darkness.

Gnostics could not reconcile the vengeful, jealous, violent, capricious, quixotic, angry god of the Old Testament to the good, compassionate, loving god Jesus (the Logos) taught in the New Testament. Their conclusion was the actions and personality of the Old Testament god matched that of the Demiurge, and since both were said to be the creator of this flawed world, they must be the same.

Deuteronomy 32

King James Version (KJV)

36 For the LORD shall judge his people, and repent himself for his servants, when he seeth that their power is gone, and there is none shut up, or left.

37 And he shall say, Where are their gods, their rock in whom they trusted,

38 Which did eat the fat of their sacrifices, and drank the wine of their drink offerings? let them rise up and help you, and be your protection.

39 See now that I, even I, am he, and there is no god with me: I kill, and I make alive; I wound, and I heal: neither is there any that can deliver out of my hand.

40 For I lift up my hand to heaven, and say, I live for ever.

41 If I whet my glittering sword, and mine hand take hold on judgment; I will render vengeance to mine enemies, and will reward them that hate me.

42 I will make mine arrows drunk with blood, and my sword shall devour flesh; and that with the blood of the slain and of the captives, from the beginning of revenges upon the enemy.

Such a creator answers the age-old questions of why there is such violence of nature and suffering in the world and why evil can go unpunished and the innocent and good are not rewarded. The purpose of Jesus was that of a servant, sent by the Supreme God, to awaken us to the truth that the world is controlled by the Demiurge, who is enslaving us to worship him, even though he is wicked and evil. Jesus was sent to draw us back to the true God and to remind us how to commune with him so as never to be deceived again.

Said another way: The All, wishing to call those who desire him into His fullness, reached out with rays of Gnosis to quicken their hearts into fervent desire for Him with a desire that is His toward us. In this way, Gnosis defeats our fate. Jesus was the courier of God's gnosis.

One of the more perfect and complete modern metaphors of Gnosticism is the movie, "The Matrix." If you take one pill you will remain comfortably oblivious to the truth, but if you decide to swallow the other pill you will awaken and be very troubled by what you see, but you will be truly free.

In one Gnostic creation story, the Archons created Adam but could not bring him to life. In other stories Adam was formed as a type of worm, unable to attain personhood. Thus, man began as an incomplete creation of a flawed, spiritually blind, and malevolent god. In this myth, the Archons were afraid that Adam might be more powerful than the Archons themselves. When they saw Adam was incapable of attaining the human state, their fears were put to rest, thus, they called that day the "Day of Rest."

Sophia saw Adam's horrid state and had compassion, because she knew she was the origin of the Archons and their evil. Sophia descended to help bring Adam out of his hopeless condition. It is this story that set the stage for the emergence of the sacred feminine force in Gnosticism that is not seen in orthodox Christianity. Sophia brought within herself the light and power of the Supreme God. Metaphorically, within the spiritual womb of Sophia was carried the life force of the Supreme God for Adam's salvation.

In the Gnostic text called, *The Apocryphon of John*, Sophia is quoted:

"I entered into the midst of the cage which is the prison of the body. And I spoke saying: 'He who hears, let him awake from his deep sleep.' Then Adam wept and shed tears. After he wiped away his bitter tears he asked: 'Who calls my name, and from where has this hope arose in me even while I am in the chains of this prison?' And I (Sophia) answered: 'I am the one who carries the pure light; I am the thought of the undefiled spirit. Arise, remember, and follow your origin, which is I, and beware of the deep sleep.'"

Sophia would later equate to the Holy Spirit as it awakened the comatose soul.

As the myth evolved, Sophia, after animating Adam, became Eve in order to assist Adam in finding the truth. She offered it to him in the form of the fruit of the tree of knowledge. To Gnostics, this was an act of deliverance.

Other stories have Sophia becoming the serpent in order to offer Adam a way to attain the truth. In either case, the fruit represented the hard sought truth, which was the knowledge of good and evil, and through that knowledge Adam could become a god. Later, the serpent would become a feminine symbol of wisdom, probably owing to the connection with Sophia. Eve, being Sophia in disguise, would become the mother and sacred feminine of us all. As Gnostic theology began to coalesce, Sophia would come to be considered a force or conduit of the Holy Spirit, in part due to the fact that the Holy Spirit was also considered a feminine and creative force from the Supreme God. The Gospel of Philip echoes this theology in verse six as follows:

In the days when we were Hebrews we were made orphans, having only our Mother. Yet when we believed in the Messiah (and became the ones of Christ), the Mother and Father both came to us. *Gospel of Philip*

As the emerging orthodox church became more and more oppressive to women, later even labeling them "occasions of sin," the Gnostics countered by raising women to equal status with men, saying Sophia was, in a sense, the handmaiden or wife of the Supreme God, making the soul of Adam her spiritual offspring.

In Gnostic cosmology the "living" world is under the control of entities called Aeons, of which Sophia is head. This means the Aeons influence or control the soul, life force, intelligence, thought, and mind. Control of the mechanical or inorganic world is given to the Archons. They rule the physical aspects of systems, regulation, limits, and order in the world. Both the ineptitude and cruelty of the Archons are reflected in the chaos and pain of the material realm.

Yaldabaoth, the lesser God that created the world, began his existence in a state that was both detached and remote from the Supreme God in aspects both spiritual and physical. Since Sophia had misused her creative force, which passed from the Supreme God to her, Sophia's creation, the Demiurge, Yaldabaoth, contained only part of the original creative spark of the Supreme Being. He was created with an imperfect nature caused by his distance in lineage and in spirit from the Divine

All or Supreme God. It is because of his imperfections and limited abilities the lesser God is also called the "Half-Maker".

The Creator God, the Demiurge, and his helpers, the Archons took the stuff of existence produced by the Supreme God and fashioned it into this material world.

Since the Demiurge (Yaldabaoth) had no memory of how he came to be alive, he did not realize he was not the true creator. The Demiurge believed he somehow created the material world by himself. The Supreme God allowed the Demiurge and Archons to remain deceived. Yet, Sophia, his mother tried to open his eyes, crying out to him, "You are not alone, Samael." (Samael – god of the blind or blind god.)

The Creator God (the Demiurge) intended the material world to be perfect and eternal, but he did not have it in himself to accomplish the feat. What comes forth from a being cannot be greater than the highest part of him, can it? The world was created flawed and transitory and we are part of it. Can we escape? The Demiurge was imperfect and evil. So was the world he created. If it was the Demiurge who created man and man is called upon to escape the Demiurge and find union with the Supreme God, is this not demanding that man becomes greater than his creator? Spiritually this seems impossible, but as many children become greater than their parents, man is expected to become greater than his maker, the Demiurge. This starts with the one fact that the Demiurge denies: the existence and supremacy of the Supreme God.

Man was created with a dual nature as the product of the material world of the Demiurge with his imperfect essence, combined with the spark of God that emanated from the Supreme God through Sophia. A version of the creation story has Sophia instructing the Demiurge to breath into Adam that spiritual power he had taken from Sophia during his creation. It was the spiritual power from Sophia that brought life to Adam.

It is this divine spark in man that calls to its source, the Supreme God, and which causes a "divine discontent," that nagging feeling that keeps us questioning if this is all there is. This spark and the feeling it gives us keeps us searching for the truth. We wish to shake ourselves and awaken to the full truth, the Gnosis, but Yaldabaoth, also called Samael, the god of the blind, has no intention of letting us see. It was to this end, to awaken man and allow him to see, the Jesus, the Logos, came.

The Creator God sought to keep man ignorant of his defective state by keeping him enslaved to the material world. By doing so, he continued to receive man's worship and servitude. He did not wish man to recognize or gain knowledge of the true Supreme God. Since he did not know or acknowledge the Supreme God, he views any attempt to worship anything else as spiritual treason.

The opposition of forces set forth in the spiritual battle over the continued enslavement of man and man's spiritual freedom set up the duality of good and evil in Gnostic theology. There was a glaring difference between the orthodox Christian viewpoint and the Gnostic viewpoint. According to Gnostics, the creator of the material world was an evil entity and the Supreme God, who was his source, was the good entity. Christians quote John 1:1 "In the beginning was the Word, and the Word was with God, and the Word was God."

According to Gnostics, only through the realization of man's true state or through death can he escape captivity in the material realm. This means the idea of salvation does not deal with original sin or blood payment. Instead, it focuses on the idea of awakening to the fullness of the truth.

According to Gnostic theology, neither Jesus nor his death can save anyone, but the truth that he came to proclaim can give people the divine, complete and perfect knowledge, which allows a person to save his or her own soul. It is the truth, or realization of the lie of the material world and its God, that sets one on a course of freedom.

There are stages to any communion with truth. One must prepare oneself. As it is written, "I will meditate for a thousand years to be enlightened in a single moment."

We must offer ourselves as a sacrifice, giving up our all for our sacred goal. In as much as the word, "sacrifice" comes from a word which means to "make holy" or "make sacred", we sacrifice our egos and preconceived ideas on the alter of knowledge. It is at this point we gain unity and individuation.

Lastly, we must commune fully with God through the knowledge, which is the fullness of God. We become the Eucharist, which means "the Thanksgiving", and through the fire of Gnosis we become the holocaust, a Latin word meaning, "the whole burnt offering." For, not being able to avoid their murder by fire, a million souls went up in smoke to the God of this world as a sacrifice. The act given the same name as the offering burned on the altar and described in the Vulgate. But now, each of us offer ourselves in the fire of Gnosis to the High and Supreme God.

To escape the earthly prison and find one's way back to the pleroma (heaven) and the Supreme God, is the soteriology (salvation doctrine) and eschatology (judgment, reward, and doctrine of heaven) of Gnosticism.

The idea that personal revelation leads to salvation may be what caused the mainline Christian church to declare Gnosticism a heresy. The church could better tolerate alternative theological views if the views did not undermine the authority of the church and its ability to control the people. Gnostic theology placed salvation in the hands of the individual through personal revelations and knowledge, excluding the need for the orthodox church and its clergy to grant salvation or absolution. This fact, along with the divergent interpretation of the creation story, which placed the creator God, Yaldabaoth or Jehovah, as the enemy of mankind, was too much for the church to tolerate. Reaction was harsh. Gnosticism was declared to be a dangerous heresy.

Gnosticism may be considered polytheistic because it espoused many "levels" of Gods, beginning with an ultimate, unknowable, Supreme God and descending as he created Sophia, and Sophia created the Demiurge (Creator God); each becoming more inferior and limited.

There is a hint of pantheism in Gnostic theology due to the fact that creation occurs because of a deterioration of the Godhead and the dispersion of the creative essence, which eventually devolves into the creation of man.

In the end, there occurs a universal reconciliation as being after being realizes the existence of the Supreme God and renounces the material world and its inferior creator.

Combined with its Christian influences, the cosmology of the Gnostics may have borrowed from the Greek philosopher, Plato, as well as from Buddhism. There are disturbing parallels between the creation myth set forth by Plato and some of those recorded in Gnostic writings.

Plato lived from 427 to 347 B.C. He was the son of wealthy Athenians and a student of the philosopher, Socrates, and the mathematician, Pythagoras. Plato himself was the teacher of Aristotle.

In Plato's cosmology, the Demiurge is an artist who imposed form on materials that already existed. The raw materials were in a chaotic and random state. The physical world must have had visible form which was put together much like a puzzle is

37

constructed. This later gave way to a philosophy which stated that all things in existence could be broken down into a small subset of geometric shapes.

In the tradition of Greek mythology, Plato's cosmology began with a creation story. The story was narrated by the philosopher Timaeus of Locris, a fictional character of Plato's making. In his account, nature is initiated by a creator deity, called the "Demiurge," a name which may be the Greek word for "craftsman" or "artisan" or, according to how one divides the word, it could also be translated as "half-maker."

The Demiurge sought to create the cosmos modeled on his understanding of the supreme and original truth. In this way he created the visible universe based on invisible truths. He set in place rules of process such as birth, growth, change, death, and dissolution. This was Plato's "Realm of Becoming." It was his Genesis. Plato stated that the internal structure of the cosmos had innate intelligence and was therefore called the World Soul. The cosmic super-structure of the Demiurge was used as the framework on which to hang or fill in the details and parts of the universe. The Demiurge then appointed his underlings to fill in the details which allowed the universe to remain in a working and balanced state. All phenomena of nature resulted from an interaction and interplay of the two forces of reason and necessity.

Plato represented reason as constituting the World Soul. The material world was a necessity in which reason acted out its will in the physical realm. The duality between the will, mind, or reason of the World Soul and the material universe and its inherent flaws set in play the duality of Plato's world and is seen reflected in the beliefs of the Gnostics.

In Plato's world, the human soul was immortal, each soul was assigned to a star. Souls that were just or good were permitted to return to their stars upon their death. Unjust souls were reincarnated to try again. Escape of the soul to the freedom of the stars and out of the cycle of reincarnation was best accomplished by following the reason and goodness of the World Soul and not the physical world, which was set in place only as a necessity to manifest the patterns of the World Soul.

Although in Plato's cosmology the Demiurge was not seen as evil, in Gnostic cosmology he was considered not only to be flawed and evil, but he was also the beginning of all evil in the material universe, having created it to reflect his own malice.

Following the path of Plato's cosmology, some Gnostics left open the possibility of reincarnation if the person had not reached the truth before his death.

In the year 13 A.D. Roman annals record the visit of an Indian king named Pandya or Porus. He came to see Caesar Augustus carrying a letter of introduction in Greek. He was accompanied by a monk who burned himself alive in the city of Athens to prove his faith in Buddhism. The event was described by Nicolaus of Damascus as, not surprisingly, causing a great stir among the people. It is thought that this was the first transmission of Buddhist teaching to the masses.

In the second century A.D., Clement of Alexandria wrote about Buddha: "Among the Indians are those philosophers also who follow the precepts of Boutta (Buddha), whom they honour as a god on account of his extraordinary sanctity." (Clement of Alexandria, "The Stromata, or Miscellanies" Book I, Chapter XV).

"Thus philosophy, a thing of the highest utility, flourished in antiquity among the barbarians, shedding its light over the nations. And afterwards it came to Greece." (Clement of Alexandria, "The Stromata, or Miscellanies").

To clarify what "philosophy" was transmitted from India to Greece, we turn to the historians Hippolytus and Epiphanius who wrote of Scythianus, a man who had visited India around 50 A.D. They report; "He brought 'the doctrine of the Two Principles.'" According to these writers, Scythianus' pupil Terebinthus called himself a Buddha. Some scholars suggest it was he that traveled to the area of Babylon and transmitted his knowledge to Mani, who later founded Manichaeism.

Adding to the possibility of Eastern influence, we have accounts of the Apostle Thomas' attempt to convert the people of Asia-Minor. If the Gnostic gospel bearing his name was truly written by Thomas, it was penned after his return from India, where he also encountered the Buddhist influences.

Ancient church historians mention that Thomas preached to the Parthians in Persia, and it is said he was buried in Edessa. Fourth century chronicles attribute the evangelization of India (Asia-Minor or Central Asia) to Thomas.

The texts of the Gospel of Thomas, which some believe predate the four gospels, has a very "Zen-like" or Eastern flavor.

Since it is widely held that the four gospels of Matthew, Mark, Luke, and John have a common reference in the basic text of Mark, it stands to reason that all follow the same general insight and language. If The Gospel of Thomas was written in his absence from the other apostles or if it was the first gospel written, one can assume it was written outside the influences common to the other gospels.

Although the codex found in Egypt is dated to the fourth century, the actual construction of the text of Thomas is placed by most Biblical scholars at about 70–150 A.D. Most agree the time of writing was in the second century A.D.

Following the transmission of the philosophy of "Two Principals," both Manichaeism and Gnosticism retained a dualistic viewpoint. The black-versus-white dualism of Gnosticism came to rest in the evil of the material world and its maker, versus the goodness of the freed soul and the Supreme God with whom it seeks union.

Oddly, the disdain for the material world and its Creator God drove Gnostic theology to far-flung extremes in attitude, beliefs, and actions. Gnostics idolize the serpent in the "Garden of Eden" story. After all, if your salvation hinges on secret knowledge the offer of becoming gods through the knowledge of good and evil sounds wonderful. So powerful was the draw of this "knowledge myth" to the Gnostics that the serpent became linked to Sophia by some sects. This can still be seen today in our medical and veterinarian symbols of serpents on poles, conveying the ancient meanings of knowledge and wisdom.

Genesis 3 (King James Version)

1 Now the serpent was more subtil than any beast of the field which the LORD God had made. And he said unto the woman, Yea, hath God said, Ye shall not eat of every tree of the garden?

2 And the woman said unto the serpent, We may eat of the fruit of the trees of the garden:

3 But of the fruit of the tree which is in the midst of the garden, God hath said, Ye shall not eat of it, neither shall ye touch it, lest ye die.

4 And the serpent said unto the woman, Ye shall not surely die:

5 For God doth know that in the day ye eat thereof, then your eyes shall be opened, and ye shall be as Gods, knowing good and evil.

It is because of their vehement struggle against the Creator God and the search for some transcendent truth, that Gnostics held the people of Sodom in high regard. The people of Sodom sought to "corrupt" the messengers sent by their enemy, the Creator God. Anything done to thwart the Demiurge and his minions was considered valiant.

Genesis 19 (King James Version)

1 And there came two angels to Sodom at even; and Lot sat in the gate of Sodom: and Lot seeing them rose up to meet them; and he bowed himself with his face toward the ground;

2 And he said, Behold now, my lords, turn in, I pray you, into your servant's house, and tarry all night, and wash your feet, and ye shall rise up early, and go on your ways. And they said, Nay; but we will abide in the street all night.

3 And he pressed upon them greatly; and they turned in unto him, and entered into his house; and he made them a feast, and did bake unleavened bread, and they did eat.

4 But before they lay down, the men of the city, even the men of Sodom, compassed the house round, both old and young, all the people from every quarter:

5 And they called unto Lot, and said unto him, Where are the men which came in to thee this night? bring them out unto us, that we may know them.

6 And Lot went out at the door unto them, and shut the door after him,

7 And said, I pray you, brethren, do not so wickedly.

8 Behold now, I have two daughters which have not known man; let me, I pray you, bring them out unto you, and do ye to them as is good in your eyes: only unto these men do nothing; for therefore came they under the shadow of my roof.

9 And they said, Stand back. And they said again, This one fellow came in to sojourn, and he will needs be a judge: now will we deal worse with thee, than with them. And they pressed sore upon the man, even Lot, and came near to break the door.

10 But the men put forth their hand, and pulled Lot into the house to them, and shut to the door.

To modern Christians, the idea of admiring the serpent, which we believe was Satan, may seem unthinkable. Supporting the idea of attacking and molesting the angels sent to Sodom to warn of the coming destruction seems appalling; but to Gnostics the real evil was the malevolent entity, the Creator God of this world. To destroy his messengers, as was the case in Sodom, would impede his mission. To obtain knowledge of good and evil, as was offered by the serpent in the garden, would set the captives free.

To awaken the inner knowledge of the true God was the battle. The material world was designed to prevent the awakening by entrapping, confusing, and distracting the spirit of man. The aim of Gnosticism was the spiritual awakening and freedom of man.

Gnostics, in the age of the early church, would preach to converts (novices) about this awakening, saying the novice must awaken the God within himself and see the trap that was the material world. Salvation came from the recognition or knowledge contained in this spiritual awakening.

Not all people are ready or willing to accept the Gnosis. Many are bound to the material world and are satisfied to be only as and where they are. These have mistaken the Creator God for the Supreme God and do not know there is anything beyond the Creator God or the material existence. These people know only the lower or earthly wisdom and not the higher wisdom above the Creator God. They are referred to as "dead."

Gnostic sects split primarily into two categories. Both branches held that those who were truly enlightened could no longer be influenced by the material world. Both divisions of Gnosticism believed that their spiritual journey could not be impeded by the material realm since the two were not only separate but in opposition. Such an attitude influenced some Gnostics toward Stoicism, choosing to abstain from the world, and others toward Epicureanism, choosing to indulge.

Major schools fell into two categories; those who rejected the material world of the Creator God, and those who rejected the laws of the Creator God. For those who rejected the world the Creator God had spawned, overcoming the material world was accomplished by partaking of as little of the world and its pleasures as possible. These followers lived very stark and ascetic lives, abstaining from meat, sex, marriage, and all things that would entice them to remain in the material realm.

Other schools believed it was their duty to simply defy the Creator God and all laws that he had proclaimed. Since the Creator God had been identified as Jehovah, God of the Jews, these followers set about to break every law held dear by Christians and Jews.

As human nature is predisposed to do, many Gnostics took up the more wanton practices, believing that nothing done in their earthly bodies would affect their spiritual lives. Whether it was excesses in sex, alcohol, food, or any other assorted debaucheries, the Gnostics were safe within their faith, believing nothing spiritually bad could come of their earthly adventures.

The actions of the Gnostics are mentioned by early Church leaders. One infamous Gnostic school is actually mentioned in the Bible, as we will read later.

The world was out of balance, inferior, and corrupt. The spirit was perfect and intact. It was up to the Gnostics to tell the story, explain the error, and awaken the world to the light of truth. The Supreme God had provided a vehicle to help in their effort. He had created a teacher of light and truth.

Since the time of Sophia's mistaken creation of the Archons, there was an imbalance in the cosmos. The Supreme God began to re-establish the balance by producing Christ to teach and save man. That left only Sophia, now in a fallen and bound state, along with the Demiurge, and the Archons to upset the cosmic equation. In this theology one might loosely equate the Supreme God to the New Testament Christian God, Demiurge to Satan, the Archons to demons, the pleroma to heaven, and Sophia to the creative or regenerative force of the Holy Spirit. This holds up well except for one huge problem. If the Jews believed that Jehovah created all things, and the Gnostic believed that the Demiurge created all things, then to the Gnostic mind, the Demiurge must be Old Testament god, Jehovah, and that made Jehovah their enemy.

For those who seek that which is beyond the material world and its flawed creator, the Supreme God has sent Messengers of Light to awaken the divine spark of the Supreme God within us. This part of us will call to the true God as deep calls to deep. The greatest and most perfect Messenger of Light was the Christ. He is also referred to as The Good, Christ, Messiah, and

The Word. He came to reveal the Divine Light to us in the form of knowledge.

According to the Gnostics, Christ came to show us our own divine spark and to awaken us to the illusion of the material world and its flawed maker. He came to show us the way back to the divine Fullness (The Supreme God). The path to enlightenment was the knowledge sleeping within each of us. Christ came to show us the Christ spirit living in each of us. Individual ignorance or the refusal to awaken our internal divine spark was the only original sin. Christ was the only Word spoken by God that could awaken us. Christ was also the embodiment of the Word itself. He was part of the original transmission from the Supreme God that took form on the earth to awaken the soul of man so that man might search beyond the material world.

One Gnostic view of the Incarnation was "docetic," which is an early heretical position that Jesus was never actually present in the flesh, but only appeared to be human. He was a spiritual being and his human appearance was only an illusion. Of course, the title of "heretical" can only be decided by the controlling authority of the time. In this case it was the church that was about to emerge under the rule of the Emperor Constantine.

Most Gnostics held that the Christ spirit indwelt the earthly Jesus at the time of his baptism by John, at which time Jesus received the name, and thus the power, of the Lord or Supreme God.

The Christ spirit departed from Jesus' body before his death. These two viewpoints remove the idea of God sacrificing himself atonement for the sins of man. The idea of atonement was not necessary in Gnostic theology since it was knowledge and not sacrifice that set one free.

Since there was a distinction in Gnosticism between the man Jesus and the Light of Christ that came to reside within him, it is not contrary to Gnostic beliefs that Mary Magdalene could have been the consort and wife of Jesus. Neither would it have been blasphemous for them to have children.

Various sects of Gnosticism stressed certain elements of their basic theology. Each had its head teachers and its special flavor of beliefs. One of the oldest types was the Syrian Gnosticism. It existed around 120 A.D. In contrast to other sects, the Syrian lacked much of the embellished mythology of Aeons, Archons, and angels.

The fight between the Supreme God and the Creator God was not eternal, though there was strong opposition to Jehovah, the Creator God. He was considered to have been the last of the seven angels who created this world out of divine material which emanated from the Supreme God. The Demiurge attempted to create man, but only created a miserable worm which the Supreme God had to save by giving it the spark of divine life. Thus man was born.

According to this sect, Jehovah, the Creator God, must not be worshiped. The Supreme God calls us to his service and presence through Christ his Son. They pursued only the unknowable Supreme God and sought to obey the Supreme Deity by abstaining from eating meat and from marriage and sex, and by leading an ascetic life. The symbol of Christ was the serpent, that attempted to free Adam and Eve from their ignorance and entrapment to the Creator God.

Another Gnostic school was the Hellenistic or Alexandrian School. These systems absorbed the philosophy and concepts of the Greeks, and the Semitic nomenclature was replaced by Greek names. The cosmology and myth had grown out of proportion and appear to our eyes to be unwieldy. Yet, this school produced two great thinkers, Basilides and Valentinus. Though born at Antioch, in Syria, Basilides founded his school in Alexandria around the year A.D. 130, where it survived for several centuries.

Valentinus first taught at Alexandria and then in Rome. He established the largest Gnostic movement around A.D. 160. This movement was founded on an elaborate mythology and a system of sexual duality of male and female interplay, both in its deities and its savior.

Tertullian wrote that between 135 A.D. and 160 A.D. Valentinus, a prominent Gnostic, had great influence in the Christian church. Valentinus ascended in church hierarchy and became a candidate for the office of bishop of Rome, the office that quickly evolved into that of Pope. He lost the election by a narrow margin. Even though Valentinus was outspoken about his Gnostic slant on Christianity, he was a respected member of the Christian community until his death and was probably a practicing bishop in a church of lesser status than the one in Rome.

The main platform of Gnosticism was the ability to transcend the material world through the possession of privileged and directly imparted knowledge. Following this doctrine, Valentinus claimed to have been instructed by a direct disciple of one of Jesus' apostles, a man by the name of Theodas.

Valentinus is considered by many to be the father of modern Gnosticism. His vision of the faith is summarized by G.R.S. Mead in the book "Fragments of a Faith Forgotten."

"The Gnosis in his hands is trying to embrace everything, even the most dogmatic formulation of the traditions of the Master. The great popular movement and its incomprehensibilities were recognized by Valentinus as an integral part of the mighty outpouring; he laboured to weave all together, external and internal, into one piece, devoted his life to the task, and doubtless only at his death perceived that for that age he was attempting the impossible. None but the very few could ever appreciate the ideal of the man, much less understand it. " (Fragments of a Faith Forgotten, p. 297)

Gnostic theology seemed to vacillate from polytheism to pantheism to dualism to monotheism, depending on the teacher and how he viewed and stressed certain areas of their creation myths.   Marcion, a Gnostic teacher, espoused differences between the God of the New Testament and the God of the Old Testament, claiming they were two separate entities. According to Marcion, the New Testament God was a good true God while the Old Testament God was an evil angel.

Although this may be a heresy, it pulled his school back into monotheism. The church, however, disowned him.

Syneros and Prepon, disciples of Marcion, postulated three different entities, carrying their teachings from monotheism into polytheism in one stroke. In their system the opponent of the good God was not the God of the Jews, but Eternal Matter, which was the source of all evil. Matter, in this system became a principal creative force. Although it was created imperfect, it could also create, having the innate intelligence of the "world soul."

Of all the Gnostic schools or sects the most famous is the Antinomian School. Believing that the Creator God, Jehovah, was evil, they sat out to disrupt all things connected to the Jewish God. This included his laws. It was considered their duty to break any law of morality, diet, or conduct given by the Jewish God, who they considered the evil Creator God. The leader of the sect was called Nicolaites. The sect existed in Apostolic times and is mentioned in the Bible.

Revelation 2 (King James Version)
5 Remember therefore from whence thou art fallen, and repent, and do the first works; or else I will come unto thee quickly, and will

remove thy candlestick out of his place, except thou repent.

6 But this thou hast, that thou hatest the deeds of the Nicolaitanes, which I also hate.

Revelation 2 (King James Version)

14 But I have a few things against thee, because thou hast there them that hold the doctrine of Balaam, who taught Balac to cast a stumbling block before the children of Israel, to eat things sacrificed unto idols, and to commit fornication.

15 So hast thou also them that hold the doctrine of the Nicolaitanes, which thing I hate.

16 Repent; or else I will come unto thee quickly, and will fight against them with the sword of my mouth.

One of the leaders of the Nocolaitanes, according to Origen, was Carpocrates, whom Tertullian called a magician and a fornicator. Carpocretes taught that one could only escape the cosmic powers by discharging one's obligations to them and disregarding their laws. The Christian church fathers, St. Justin, Irenaeus, and Eusebius wrote that the reputation of these men (the Nicolaitanes), brought infamy upon the whole race of Christians.

Although Gnostic sects varied, they had certain points in common. These commonalities included salvation through special knowledge, and the fact that the world was corrupt as it was created by an evil God.

According to Gnostic theology, nothing can come from the material world that is not flawed. Because of this, Gnostics did not believe that Christ could have been a corporeal being. Thus, there must be some separation or distinction between Jesus, as a man, and Christ, as a spiritual being born from the Supreme, unrevealed, and eternal God.

To closer examine this theology, we turn to Valentinus, the driving force of early Gnosticism, for an explanation. Valentinus divided Jesus Christ into two very distinct parts; Jesus, the man, and Christ, the anointed spiritual messenger of God. These two forces met in the moment of Baptism when the Spirit of God came to rest on Jesus and the Christ power entered his body.

Here Gnosticism runs aground on its own theology, for if the spiritual cannot mingle with the material then how can the Christ spirit inhabit a body? The result of the dichotomy was a schism within Gnosticism. Some held to the belief that the specter of Jesus was simply an illusion produced by Christ himself to enable him to do his work on earth. It was not real, not matter, not corporeal, and did not actually exist as a physical body would. Others came to believe that Jesus must have been a specially prepared vessel and was the perfect human body formed by the very essence of the plumora (heaven). It was this path of thought that allowed Jesus to continue as human, lover, and father.

Jesus, the man, became a vessel containing the Light of God, called Christ. In the Gnostic view we all could and should become Christs, carrying the Truth and Light of God. We are all potential vehicles of the same Spirit that Jesus held within him when he was awakened to the Truth.

The suffering and death of Jesus then took on much less importance in the Gnostic view, as Jesus was simply part of the corrupt world and was suffering the indignities of this world as any man would. Therefore, from their viewpoint, he could have been married and been a father without disturbing Gnostic theology in the least.

The Gnostic texts seem to divide man into parts, although at times the divisions are somewhat unclear. The divisions alluded to may include the soul, which is the will of man; the spirit, which is depicted as wind or air (pneuma) and contains the holy spark that is the spirit of God in man; and the material human form, the body. The mind of man sits as a mediator between the soul, or will, and the spirit, which is connected to God.

Without the light of the truth, the spirit is held captive by the Demiurge, which enslaves man. This entrapment is called "sickness." It is this sickness that the Light came to heal and then to set us free. The third part of man, his material form, was considered a weight, an anchor, and a hindrance, keeping man attached to the corrupted earthly realm.

As we read the text, we must realize that Gnosticism conflicted with traditional Christianity. Overall theology can rise and fall upon small words and terms. If Jesus was not God, his death and thus his atonement meant nothing. His suffering meant nothing. Even the resurrection meant nothing, if one's view of Jesus was that he was not human to begin with, as was true with some Gnostics.

For the Gnostics, resurrection of the dead was unthinkable since flesh as well as all matter is destined to perish. According to Gnostic theology, there was no resurrection of the flesh, but only of the soul. How the soul would be resurrected was explained differently by various Gnostic groups, but all denied the resurrection of the body. To the enlightened Gnostic the actual person was the spirit who used the body as an instrument to survive in the material world but did not identify with it. This belief is echoed in the Gospel of Thomas.

29. Jesus said: If the flesh came into being because of spirit, it is a marvel, but if spirit came into being because of the body, it would be a marvel of marvels. I marvel indeed at how great wealth has taken up residence in this poverty.

Owing to the Gnostic belief of such a separation of spirit and body, it was thought that the Christ spirit within the body of Jesus departed the body before the crucifixion. Others said the body was an illusion and the crucifixion was a sham perpetrated by an eternal spirit on the men that sought to kill it. Lastly, some suggested that Jesus deceived the soldiers into thinking he was dead. The resurrection under this circumstance became a lie which allowed Jesus to escape and live on in anonymity, hiding, living as a married man, and raising a family until his natural death.

Think of the implications to the orthodox Christian world if the spirit of God departed from Jesus as it fled and laughed as the body was crucified. This is the implication of the Gnostic interpretation of the death of Jesus when he cries out, "My power, my power, why have you left me," as the Christ spirit left his body before his death. What are the ramifications to the modern Christian if the Creator God, the Demiurge, is more evil than his creation? Can a Creation rise above its creator? Is it possible for man to find the spark within himself that calls to the Supreme God and free himself of his evil creator?

Although, in time, the creation myth and other Gnostic differences began to be swept under the rug, it was the division between Jesus and the Christ spirit that put them at odds with the emerging orthodox church. At the establishment of the doctrine of the trinity, the mainline church firmly set a divide between themselves and the Gnostics.

To this day there is a battle raging in the Christian world as believers and seekers attempt to reconcile today's Christianity to the sect of the early Christian church called, "Gnosticism."

Carl Jung and the Application of Gnosticism

A little know fact is the great father of modern psychology, Carl G. Jung, had great interest in Gnosticism, and went so far as to purchase an ancient codex.

Gilles Quispel is a distinguished professor of Early Christianity who was born in Rotterdam, Holland in 1916. As a young man he obtained a doctorate in literature and the humanities and went on to research and teach about the early Gnostics. He describes his first meeting with Jung in 1944 in Ascona, Switzerland and how he gained the help of Jung and C.A. Meier to retrieve a valuable Gnostic text from the black market. This text had been part of a larger cache of ancient documents found in 1945 buried in a jar in Egypt near Nag Hammadi. Scholars consider these documents extremely valuable as the texts were from the first century C.E. and contained unknown sayings of Jesus including a book titled, "The Gospel of Truth". The lost text was retrieved and named the *Jung Codex*.

It may be of interest to note the connection between the ancient Gnostics and modern psychology.

Stephan A. Hoeller wrote, in his article, "**C. G. Jung and the Alchemical Renewal,**" the following:

Jung's "first love" among esoteric systems was Gnosticism. From the earliest days of his scientific career until the time of his death, his dedication to the subject of Gnosticism was relentless. As early as August, 1912, Jung intimated in a letter to Freud that he had an intuition that the essentially feminine-toned archaic wisdom of the Gnostics, symbolically called *Sophia*, was destined to re-enter modern Western culture by way of depth-psychology. Subsequently, he stated to Barbara Hannah that when he discovered the writings of the ancient Gnostics, "I felt as if I had at last found a circle of friends who understood me."

The circle of ancient friends was a fragile one, however. Very little reliable, first-hand information was available to Jung within which he could have found the world and spirit of such past Gnostic luminaries as Valentinus, Basilides, and others. The fragmentary, and possibly mendacious, accounts of Gnostic teachings and practices appearing in the works of such heresy-hunting church fathers as Irenaeus and Hippolytus were a far cry from the wealth of archetypal lore available to us today in the Nag Hammadi collection. Of primary sources, the remarkable *Pistis Sophia* was one of very few available to Jung in translation, and his appreciation of this work was so great that he made a special effort to seek out the translator, the then aged and impecunious George R. S. Mead, in London to convey to him his great gratitude. Jung continued to explore Gnostic lore with great diligence, and his own personal matrix of inner experience became so affinitized to Gnostic imagery that he wrote the only published document of his great transformational crisis, *The Seven Sermons to the Dead*, using purely Gnostic terminology and mythologems of the system of Basilides.

In all this devoted study, Jung was disturbed by one principal difficulty: The ancient Gnostic myths and traditions were some seventeen or eighteen hundred years old, and no living link seemed to exist that might join them to Jung's own time. (There is some minimal and obscure evidence indicating that Jung was aware of a few small and secretive Gnostic groups in France and Germany, but their role in constituting such a link did not seem firmly enough established.) As far as Jung could discern, the tradition that might have connected the Gnostics with the present seemed to have been broken. However, his intuition (later justified by painstaking research) disclosed to him that the chief link connecting later ages with the Gnostics was in fact none other than alchemy. While his primary interest at this time was Gnosticism, he was already aware of the relevance of alchemy to his concerns. Referring to his intense inner experiences occurring between 1912 and 1919 he wrote:

First I had to find evidence for the historical prefiguration of my own inner experiences. That is to say, I had to ask myself, "Where have my particular premises already occurred in history?" If I had not succeeded in finding such evidence, I would never have been able to substantiate my ideas. Therefore, my encounter with alchemy was decisive for me, as it provided me with the historical basis which I hitherto lacked.

In 1926 Jung had a remarkable dream. He felt himself transported back into the seventeenth century, and saw himself as an alchemist, engaged in the *opus*, or great work of alchemy. Prior to this time, Jung, along with other psychoanalysts, was intrigued and taken aback by the tragic fate of Herbert Silberer, a disciple of Freud, who in 1914 published a work dealing largely with the psychoanalytic implications of alchemy. Silberer, who upon proudly presenting his book to his master Freud, was coldly rebuked by him, became despondent and ended his life by suicide, thus becoming what might be called the first martyr to the cause of a psychological view of alchemy.

Now it all came together, as it were. The Gnostic Sophia was about to begin her triumphal return to the arena of modern thought, and the psychological link connecting her and her modern devotees would be the long despised, but about to be rehabilitated, symbolic discipline of alchemy. The recognition had come. Heralded by a dream, the role of alchemy as the link connecting ancient Gnosticism with modern psychology, as well as Jung's role in reviving this link, became apparent. As Jung was to recollect later:

[Alchemy] represented the historical link with Gnosticism, and . . . a continuity therefore existed between past and present. Grounded in the natural philosophy of the Middle Ages, alchemy formed the bridge on the one hand into the past, to Gnosticism, and on the other into the future, to the modern psychology of the unconscious.

End of quotation -

According to Marsha West, Carl Jung has been called the "Father of the re-birth of Gnosticism also called Neo-Gnosticism. Dr. Satinover comments, "One of the most powerful modern forms of Gnosticism is without question Jungian psychology, both within or without the Church."

Edward Moore wrote, "Carl Jung, drawing upon Gnostic mythical schemas, identified the objectively oriented consciousness with the material or "fleshly" part of humankind — that is, with the part of the human being that is, according to the Gnostics, bound up in the cosmic cycle of generation and decay, and subject to the bonds of fate and time (cf. *Apocryphon of John* [Codex II] 28:30). The human being who identifies him/herself with the objectively existing world comes to construct a personality, a sense of self, that is, at base, fully dependent upon the ever-changing structures of temporal existence. The resulting lack of any sense of permanence, of autonomy, leads such an individual to experience anxieties of all kinds, and eventually to shun the mysterious and collectively meaningful patterns of human existence in favor of a private and stifling subjective context, in the confines of which life plays itself out in the absence of any reference to a greater plan or scheme. Hopelessness, atheism, and despair, are the results of such an existence. This is not the natural end of the human being, though; for, according to Jung (and the Gnostics) the temporally constructed self is not the true self. The true self is the supreme consciousness existing and persisting beyond all space and time. Jung calls this the *pure consciousness* or Self, in contradistinction to the "ego consciousness" which is the temporally constructed and maintained *form* of a discrete existent (cf. C.G. Jung, "Gnostic Symbols of the Self," in *The Gnostic Jung* 1992, pp. 55-92). This latter form of "worldly" consciousness the Gnostics identified with soul (*psukhê*), while the pure or true Self they identified with spirit (*pneuma*) — that is, mind relieved of its temporal contacts and context. This distinction had an important career in Gnostic thought, and was adopted by St. Paul, most notably in his doctrine of the spiritual resurrection (1 Corinthians 15:44). The psychological or empirical basis of this view, which soon turns into a metaphysical or onto-theological attitude, is the recognized inability of the human mind to achieve its grandest designs while remaining subject to the rigid law and order of a disinterested and aloof cosmos. The spirit-soul distinction (which of course translates into, or perhaps presupposes, the more fundamental mind-body distinction) marks the beginning of a transcendentalist and soteriological attitude toward the cosmos and temporal existence in general."

End Quote

In August 1957, Jung gave a series of filmed interviews for the University of Houston. The following is part of the transcript of the fourth interview with Dr. Richard I. Evans:

"I got more and more respectful of archetypes, and now, by Jove, that thing should be taken into account. That is an enormous factor, very important for our further development and for our well-being. It was, of course, difficult to know where to begin, because it is such an enormously extended field. So the next question I asked myself was, "Now where in the world has anybody been busy with that problem?" And I found nobody had, except a peculiar spiritual movement that went together with the beginnings of Christianity, namely Gnosticism. That was the first thing, actually, that I saw, that the Gnostics were concerned with the problem of archetypes. They made a peculiar philosophy of it, as everybody makes a peculiar philosophy of it when he comes across it naïvely and doesn't know that the archetypes are structural elements of the unconscious psyche.

The Gnostics lived in the first, second, and third centuries. And what was in between? Nothing. And now, today, we suddenly fall into that hole and are confronted with the problems of the collective unconscious which were the same then two thousand years ago - and we are not prepared to meet that problem. I was always looking for something in between, you know, something that linked that remote past with the present moment. And I found to my amazement it was alchemy, which is understood to be a history of chemistry. It is, one might almost say, anything but that. It is a peculiar spiritual or philosophical movement. The alchemists called themselves philosophers, like the Gnostics. And then I read the whole accessible literature, Latin and Greek. I studied it because it was enormously interesting. It is the mental work of seventeen hundred years, in which is stored up all they could make out about the nature of the archetypes, in a peculiar way, that's true - it is not simple. Most of the texts haven't been published since the Middle Ages; the last editions date from the middle or end of the seventeenth century, practically all in Latin. Some texts are in Greek, not a few very important ones. That gave me no end of work, but the result was most satisfactory, because it showed me the development of our unconscious relations to the collective unconscious and the variations our consciousness has undergone, and why the unconscious is concerned with these mythological images. ..."

To piece this together into modern psychology we must remember that Carl Jung was formulating his ideas of psychology and religious mythos using Gnosticism as one of his favorite "jumping off points" to look at how individuals must integrate all sides of their psyches, with both good and evil, into the whole. Since myths are the subconscious symbols of spiritual reality, myths show in story form a path to wholeness of the psyche. The psyche is the gateway to the spirit and must be integrated and complete before the spirit can be freely accessed. Jung called this process of the integrate of the various parts of the psyche or soul and the integration of soul and spirit "individuation". He seemed to have gleaned this idea from the theology and mythos of the Gnostic, which he saw as a deep and intuitive application of this idea of integration and wholeness.

This idea of knowledge and wholeness being equated to salvation is not a new one. The word translated as "salvation" in the New Testament has as one of its main meanings "wholeness".

The Greek word: sōtēria, noun, Strong's # 4991, is used 45 times, commonly translated in the KJV as salvation.

Its root word is sōtēr, a noun also, Strong's # 4990, is used 24 times, commonly translated in the KJV as savior.

Its root word is sōzō, a verb, Strong's # 4982, is used 110 times, commonly translated in the KJV as save 93 times, make whole 9 times, heal 3 times, be whole 2 times, and misc. words 3 times.

In the contextual usages of the verb sōzō, the root word for both nouns sōtēr and sōtēria, had a meaning to Middle-Easterners 2,000 years ago in a sense of therapeutic restoration, in the sense of "healing", "being healed", "made whole", "kept whole", or "kept from being made unwhole".

The following verse references show sōzō to mean "make whole" or "keep whole", and shows its deeper and true meaning, than simply "saved". Since the verb sōzō is the root of sōtēr, translated savior, and sōtēria, translated salvation, then the deeper meaning of sōtēr would be, one who makes whole, and the deeper meaning of sōtēria would be wholeness.

Mat. 9:21, "if perhaps I may only touch the garment of him, I shall be made whole!"

Mat. 9:22, "the belief of you has made you whole."

Mat. 27:40, "keep whole yourself!"

Mat. 27:42, "he made whole others; himself he is absolutely not inherently powered to keep whole."

Mat. 27:49, "let us see if Elijah comes, keeping him whole."

Mark 3:4, (about the man with the withered hand) "Is it permitted on the sabbaths to do good, or to do evil; to make whole a soul, or to destroy [a soul]?"

Mark 5:23, "having come, you may put the hand to her in order that she may be made whole?"

Mark 5:28, "If perhaps I may touch even the garments of him, I shall be made whole!"

Mark 5:34, "Daughter, the belief of you has made whole you."

Mark 6:56, and as many as perhaps touched him were made whole.

Mark 10:52, "Go, the belief of you has made whole you."

Mark 15:30, "keep whole yourself, having come down from the stake."

Mark 15:31, "He made whole others; himself he is absolutely not inherently powered to keep whole."

Luke 6:9, (about the man with the withered hand) "Is it permitted on the sabbath to do good or to do evil, to make whole a soul or to destroy [a soul]?"

Luke 7:50, "The belief of you has made whole you."

Luke 8:12, "then comes the devil and lifts away the Word (logon) from the heart of them, in order that having not believed [the Word] they may [not] be made whole."

Luke 8:36, … and the ones having seen reported to them how the one having been demonized was made whole.

Luke 8:48, "Daughter, the belief of you has made whole you."

Luke 8:50, "Fear not, only believe, and she shall be made whole."

Luke 17:19, "the belief of you has made whole you."

Luke 18:42, "Look up! The belief of you has made whole you."

Luke 19:10, "Because the son of the mortal came to seek and make whole the destroyed one."

Luke 23:35, "He made whole others; if this one is the Christ, [let him] keep whole himself."

Luke 23:37, "If you are the king of the Judeans, keep whole yourself."

Luke 23:39, "Are you absolutely not the Christ? Keep whole yourself and us."

*Acts 4:9, (refering to the good deed done to the lame man, Acts 3:6-7) "if we be judged up... in what [means] this one has been made whole,"
*Acts 4:10, "...in this one's [name], this one has stood in sight of you, healthy (hugiēs)
*Acts 4:12, "And there is absolutely not in any other, the wholeness (sōtēria); because there is absolutely not another name under the heaven, the [name] having been given among mortals, in which it is necessary for you to be made whole."

Moreover, it is actually up to us, each one personally, to be responsible for his or her wholeness. Keeping in mind that wholeness equates to salvation in the Gnostic sense, since it is brought about by deep knowledge imparted by God through Jesus, which brings insight and when applied, wholeness.

Phillippians 2:12 Amplified Bible -
Therefore, my dear ones, as you have always obeyed [my suggestions], so now, not only [with the enthusiasm you would show] in my presence but much more because I am absent, **workout** (cultivate, carry **out** to the goal, and fully

complete) **your own salvation** with reverence and awe and trembling (self-distrust, with serious caution, tenderness of conscience, watchfulness against temptation, timidly shrinking from whatever might offend God and discredit the name of Christ)

Now, we see the connection between "sin" and salvation. The word for "sin" means, "missing the mark." It is not some horrible deed, but the aim of psychological and spiritual wholeness that has missed its target. Actions coming from this condition are simply commentary, just as the fire of gnosis is a commentary to wholeness.

Carl Jung saw the delineation of types in Gnostic mythos, and thus the way to distinguish them. He saw that each type had its own psychological strengths and weaknesses. These weaknesses were due to a lack of integration of certain segments of functions into the psyche as a whole.

The ideas of archetypes, personality types, and individuation would give birth to the Jungian archetypes and led to the MBTI.

The purpose of the Myers-Briggs Type Indicator® (MBTI®) personality inventory is to make the theory of psychological types described by C. G. Jung understandable and useful in people's lives. The theory is that random variation in the behavior is actually quite orderly and consistent, being due to basic differences in the ways individuals use their perception and judgment.

Perception is the way we become aware of things, people, happenings, or ideas. Judgment involves all the ways of coming to conclusions about what has been perceived. If people differ systematically in what they perceive and in how they reach conclusions, and differ correspondingly in their reactions and motivations then these differences, if systematic, can be classified into major categories he called archetypes.

On the subject of Jung's idea of individuation, Martha Blake writes, "One of the main tenets of Jungian psychology is the concept of Individuation. Individuation is striving for wholeness of the personality. Jung adopted the term from Aristotle and others who wrote of the principium individuation is, the process by which the general becomes ever more particular as it develops. Each individual has an opportunity for development that is unique. The terms individual and individuation are not synonymous. One individual sunflower is slightly different from the next, but one individual human is noticeably different from the next. The physical manifestation of two sunflowers and two human beings create individual differences. However, human beings also have personalities and each human personality is often vastly different from the others, with considerable differences in consciousness.

Jung noticed that sometimes a person may exhibit more than one personality. A man acts one way behind the desk and another way behind the wheel, or a woman is experienced one way by her colleagues and another way by her family. Jung thought that such alternate personalities residing within one person revealed unconscious parts of the human psyche that lie just below the surface of awareness and strive for expression. Becoming aware of those unconscious parts, owning them as aspects of one's humanity, and more fully developing the personality is the process Jung named "individuation." The developmental form of individuation occurs naturally in the course of a lifetime. The assisted form of individuation is the more deliberate attempt to consciously strive for wholeness. Individuation is always to some extent opposed to collective norms, since it means separation and differentiation from the general and a building up of the particular — not a particularity that is sought out, but one that is already ingrained in the psychic condition. The opposition to the collective norm, however, is only apparent, since closer examination shows that the individual standpoint is not antagonistic to it, but only differently oriented.

Each individual human is a separate being. The more the ego is involved in the process of individuation, the greater the opportunity for the pursuit of wholeness. Someone who is individuating is consciously striving for wholeness by extending consciousness and assimilating unconscious aspects of personality. Life creates a set of circumstances, consciousness creates an ego with a capacity for awareness, and memory stores an experience. When the ego is assisted to attend to unconscious contents that intrude on consciousness, individuation may be more pronounced, and the personality more whole.

Jung's focus on the individual movement toward wholeness leaves us with many questions about developmental movements in collectives. Jung acknowledged that within analytical dyads, the interactions could further the individuation of both analysand and analyst. It is a small step from an analytical dyad in which the analyst facilitates an assisted individuation of the analysand to a family group with its mixture of developmental stages, conscious and unconscious interactions in which the parents may be more conscious than the children. Members of a family simultaneously experience a strong pull toward the collective of the family and a push toward the developmental form of individuation of the individual. The observation of the dynamics of small groups is in many ways similar to the work of the family systems practitioners. In addition, some Jungian analysts have explored the relationship between the process of individuation and participation as a member of a group.

In a 1983 article entitled "Individuation and Group," Jungian analyst Robert Strubel reviewed Jung's position on the individual, the collective, adaptation, and individuation. Strubel recalls Jung's position on the collective as it relates to groups:

The social attitude does not come into operation in the dialectical relationship between patient and doctor, and may therefore remain in an unadapted state…

The danger of individual analysis is the neglect of social adaptation.

Statements like these suggest that Jung experienced adaptation and individuation as opposites, or at least appreciated the tensions between them

The **Myers-Briggs Type Indicator (MBTI)** assessment is a psychometric questionnaire designed to measure preferences in how people perceive the world and make decisions. These preferences were extrapolated from the theory of types proposed by Jung and first published in his 1921 book *Psychological Types* (English edition, 1923)

In all of Jung's work, the most important and most often stressed ideas were those of wholeness and self-awareness. This, the Gnostics called awakening.

The Gnostic myth did not have to be true in the strict sense of having actually happened to speak to our inner calling. Myths are stories designed to convey, through characters and events, a deeper meaning than could be conveyed with explanations or information. It is the myth that acts as a vehicle to the power of the idea, which affects us. To use the power of the myth we must understand and internalize the meanings, then apply the wisdom to life.

The historicity of the myth is of little concern. To illustrate this point let us look at a passage from the Bible.

Matthew 27: [50] Jesus, when he had cried again with a loud voice, yielded up the ghost. [51] And, behold, the veil of the temple was rent in twain from the top to the bottom; and the earth did quake, and the rocks rent; [52] And the graves were opened; and many bodies of the saints which slept arose,

⁵³ And came out of the graves after his resurrection, and went into the holy city, and appeared unto many.

With apologies to fundamentalists, this account is likely a non-event. If this were true such an abnormal and amazing event it would have been reported, not only by other apostles but also by the historians of the time. Indeed, the bizarre happening would have been written down by anyone who could write. The historicity of the story is not the issue. The story conveys a powerful message, which is impossible to transmit by simply saying, "Jesus died and I think he somehow gave life to the world." The event in this myth was powerful enough to impart life even to the dead. On a personal level the story tells us that we have this life inside us that will continue after death and has the power to change the very nature of life, especially our own life.

So it is with Gnosticism, or any other religion for that matter. Information engages only the mind, but a story of a mythic construct engages the emotion and intuition as well. The story must be such that we can see our own storyline in it. It must convey lessons or hope. It must do so in such a way that it moves the person to understand the potential to avoid or overcome obstacles, either internal or external.

Taking one of the more expansive Gnostic creation stories for example, we may ask, do we actually believe God created Barbelo and Barbelo produced Sophia and Sophia produced Yaldabaoth the Demiurge and the Demiurge made the world and us and has entrapped us into worshipping him by not telling us about the real God? Well, no. Many Gnostic Christians did not rely on Plato's myths. Certainly, Thomas did not mention these stories. Thomas addresses only the underlying meaning. Thomas may allude to basic components to signify a way of healing and a map back to God. This self-awareness, this truth, this wholeness is achieved only by being brutally honest with ourselves. We must be authentic and authentically honest. Integration, individuation, and a deeper truth will arise. This is the Gnosis, which leads to freedom.

I invite the reader to know the overall Gnostic mythos only to understand references made to events and characters in order to intuit their meanings. Most Gnostic branches have more limited creation myths, but all must transmit a story with spiritual lessons and undertones.

We must see that we have the potential to be each and every character in the myth.

We are Sophia, who wished to create but does not wait to be united with God and whole. We are Sophia, who is wisdom but disconnected. She created outside the state of wholeness and her creation was destructive.

We are Sophia whole and connected, who gave Adam the spirit of God and raised him out of his worm-like state.

We are the Demiurge. We are blind to our own limitations, arrogant and lost. We may have the divine spark within us but until we see the truth we will misuse our gift. We are our own god, ignoring the warnings of those more wise. As the Demiurge, whose name is Yaldabaoth, ignored Sophia, his mother, as she called to him, "You are not alone, Samael (god of the blind, or blind god)." We are so blind and arrogant we do not realize we are not united with our creator. We are not whole. We are not God.

We are the Christ spirit, not only whole and restored, but now anointed and sent from our source to aid others on their path back to the divine flame of Gnosis.

It was this idea of integration and wholeness that Jung gleaned from Gnosticism. He called it "individuation".

Jolande Jacobi, a Jungian analyst, writes in her book entitled <u>The Way of Individuation</u>, "Like a seed growing into a tree, life unfolds stage by stage. Triumphant ascent, collapse, crises, failures, and new beginnings strew the way. It is the path trodden by the great majority of mankind, as a rule unreflectingly, unconsciously, unsuspectingly, following its labyrinthine windings from birth to death in hope and longing. It is hedged about with struggle and suffering, joy and sorrow, guilt and error, and nowhere is there security from catastrophe. For as soon as a man tries to escape every risk and prefers to experience life only in his head, in the form of ideas and fantasies, as soon as he surrenders to opinions of 'how it ought to be' and, in order not to make a false step, imitates others whenever possible, he forfeits the chance of his own independent development. Only if he treads the path bravely and flings himself into life, fearing no struggle and no exertion and fighting shy of no experience, will he mature his personality more fully than the man who is ever trying to keep to the safe side of the road."

We are born of wisdom yet unrealized and of divine power, yet undiscovered. We were created outside the "fullness," but the fullness is within us, waiting, calling. Deep within there is a divine discontent. We are homesickness for a place beyond where and what we are now. Fear and attachment hold us, but the gnosis is waiting on the other side. It is transcendental consciousness brought about by a realization sparked to flame by God, from his grace, as he answers the pleading of our hearts. This is the place where angels sing in silence. This is beyond religion. Religion is made up of commands, resulting only in ethics, but gnosis changes the heart. The change is the opus. Our magnum opus is to lay aside our ego and the fear that besets us, to step outside ourselves and become one, both with our true spiritual identities, and with God in his wonderful fullness. This is the peace that passes understanding. This is the Kingdom of heaven. This is what Carl Jung called, "Individuation."

There is something in the human psyche that struggles to produce what Jung refers to as the "true personality." This struggle to bring about the birth of one's "true personality," which is a fully integrated and healthy personality, is the basis for what Jung called the process of individuation. We are involved in a process of bridging the gap between the various parts of the archetypal pieces within us. The world of the unconscious and the everyday world of ego-consciousness must be brought together, in order to realize the potentialities of one's individual psyche. In short, we must identify the various mental, emotional and spiritual elements that are part of the whole person we are intended to be. We must learn to embrace each and every part, making each part healthy. We must integrate all of the healthy pieces into a healthy wholeness.

Gnosis reveals our state of being and kingdom of heaven.
Awareness of our state urges us to seek and identify the estranged and unhealthy pieces of ourselves.
Imparted wisdom allows us the embrace our totality and bring balance, integration and health.
Only the real and total being can enter into the kingdom.

Identify – embrace – integrate – enter into salvation.

In the Gospel of Thomas the words of Jesus point toward the knowledge or gnosis that brings about the realization that we are fallen beings and unsaved creatures. We are unsaved and fallen, not because a long-dead relative broke a law or religious code in the antediluvian past, but because we have allowed ourselves to become "dis-integrated." The disintegration must stop and we must become whole once more. Health and wholeness – this is the real meaning of salvation.

The parables of Jesus are designed, like the Zen koan, to go past the logical mind and engage emotion and intuition to bring forth a fuller understanding. This is the power of the

Gospel of Thomas with it's one hundred and fourteen saying, each one aimed like an arrow, at the heart of the matter.

Let us read these texts and do as the ancient Gnostics commanded. Wake up! Heal yourself! Seek the Christ within you! Let the oil flow down! Let the Word be heard! Let the Light show you the Truth! Become the Christ you are! Give birth to what is inside you! Let the sleeper awaken!

Returning our view to that of the Gospel of Thomas, the book you hold contains the Coptic and Greek translations of The Gospel of Thomas. Presented herein are the result of a gestalt brought about by contrasting and comparing all of the foremost translations, where the best phrasing was chosen to follow the intent and meaning of the text.

Because there are differences between the Coptic manuscript and the Greek fragments of Thomas, each verse will have the following format for the reader to view; The Coptic text will be presented first, since we have the entire Gospel in this language. The Greek text will come next. If there is not a second rendition of the verse the reader may assume there was no Greek fragment found for that verse or the Greek version of the verse was identical to the Coptic version. Lastly, obvious parallels found in the Bible are listed.

Let us keep in mind that some of the differences between the translations of the Greek and Coptic may be attributed in part to the choice of word or phrase of those translating. It is the difference in overall meaning of verses between Coptic and Greek on which we should focus.

In the document to follow, the Gospel of Thomas will appear as a bold text. If there are other relevant but divergent interpretations of phrases in Thomas, they are included in parenthesis. Any parallels of text or meaning that appear in the Bible are placed below the verse in italicized text. Author's notes are in regular text. In this way the reader can easily identify which body of work is being referenced and observe how they fit together.

Let us begin.

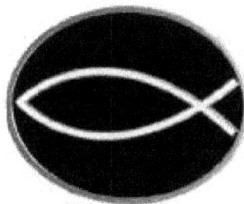

The Gnostic Gospel Of Thomas

These are the secret sayings which the living Jesus has spoken and Judas who is also Thomas (the twin) (Didymos Judas Thomas) wrote.

"The Living Jesus" could mean the Jesus living after the resurrection or the Jesus living through his sayings.

1. And he said: Whoever finds the interpretation of these sayings will not taste death.

   1. He said to them: Whoever discovers the interpretation of these words shall never taste death.

Who apprehends the deeper truths of these saying shall live.

John 8:51 Very truly I tell you, whoever keeps my word will never see death.

2. Jesus said: Let he who seeks not stop seeking until he finds, and when he finds he will be amazed (troubled), and when he has been amazed he will marvel (be astonished) and he will reign over all and in reigning, he will find rest.

2. Jesus said: Let he who seeks not stop until he finds, and when he finds he shall wonder and in wondering he shall reign, and in reigning he shall find rest.

One Greek version adds, "The reign of the one who has obtained gnosis results in rest."

When the spiritual sight sees the truth their you will be troubled that you have not seen what is so obvious before. You will be troubled that things are very different than you thought they were. You will be troubled at how simple and clear the truth has become when it was hidden so deeply a moment before.

Clement of Alexandria: "Being baptized, we are illuminated; illuminated we become sons; being made sons, we are made perfect; being made perfect, we are made immortal." (*Instructor*, 1.6.26.1)

2 Timothy 2:11-12: Trustworthy is the saying, If we have died with him, we shall also live with him; if we have endured, we shall reign with him.

3. Jesus said: If those who lead you say to you: Look, the Kingdom is in the sky, then the birds of the sky would enter before you. If they say to you: It is in the sea, then the fish of the sea would enter ahead you. But the Kingdom of God exists within you and it exists outside of you. Those who come to know (recognize) themselves will find it, and when you come to know yourselves you will become known and you will realize that you are the children of the Living Father. Yet if you do not come to know yourselves then you will dwell in poverty and it will be you who are that poverty.

3. Jesus said, If those who lead you say, "See, the Kingdom is in the sky," then the birds of the sky will precede you. If they say to you, "It is under the earth," then the fish of the sea will precede you. Rather, the Kingdom of God is inside of you, and it is outside of you.

Those who come to know themselves will find it; and when you come to know yourselves, you will understand that it is

you who are the sons of the living Father. But if you will not know yourselves, you dwell in poverty and it is you who are that poverty.

The image is of a person being poverty itself, as opposed to simply being poor. Imagine a deeply impoverished setting. You are that squalor.

An unexamined life is not worth living.

The kingdom of heaven is hidden and manifest at the same time, according to other sayings, indicating a deeper meaning than most experience.

Luke 17:20 And when he was demanded of by the Pharisees, when the kingdom of God should come, he answered them and said, The kingdom of God cometh not with observation: Neither shall they say, Lo here! Lo there! For, behold, the kingdom of God is within you.

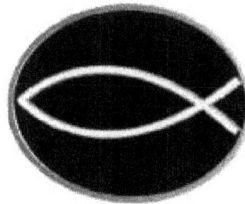

4. Jesus said: The person of old age will not hesitate to ask a

little child of seven days about the place of life, and he will live. For many who are first will become last, (and the last will be first). And they will become one and the same.

4. Jesus said: Let the old man who has lived many days not hesitate to ask the child of seven days about the place of life; then he will live. For many that are first will be last, and last will be first, and they will become a single one.

On the eighth day a Jewish boy is circumcised. The seventh day indicates he has not been circumcised yet and is still closer to God than the seeker. Several Gnostic books have Jesus appearing as a child.

The Gospel according to Thomas used by the Naassenes says: "He who seeks me will find me in children from seven years old; for there in the fourteenth age, having been hidden, I shall become manifest." (*Hidden Records of the Life of Jesus*, p. 243)

Mark 9:35-37 He sat down, called the twelve, and said to them: Whoever wants to be first must be last of all and servant of all. Then he took a little child and put it among them, and taking it in his arms, he said to them: Whoever welcomes one such child in my name welcomes me, and whoever welcomes me welcomes not me but the one who sent me.

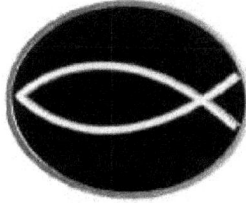

5. Jesus said: Recognize what is in front of your face, and what has been hidden from you will be revealed to you. For there is nothing hidden which will not be revealed (become manifest), and nothing buried that will not be raised.

5. Jesus said: Know what is in front of your face and what is hidden from you will be revealed to you.
For there is nothing hidden that will not be revealed.

The statement regarding things buried and raised does not appear in other than Greek texts. Since Gnostics hold little to no value in the resurrection as relating to salvation it is likely not referencing that. Things which are hidden and hiding in plain sight, just below the surface of our perception. Once you seek it you can never not-see it again.

"Understand what is in front of your face, and then what is hidden from you will be disclosed to you." (*The Gospel of Thomas: The Hidden Sayings of Jesus*, p. 71)

Mark 4:22 For there is nothing hid, except to be made manifest; nor is anything secret, except it come to light.

Luke 12:2 Nothing is covered up that will not be revealed, or hidden that will not be known.

Matthew 10:26 So have no fear of them; for nothing is covered up that will not be uncovered, and nothing secret that will not become known.

6. His Disciples asked Him, they said to him: How do you want us to fast, and how will we pray? And how will we be charitable (give alms), and what laws of diet will we maintain?

Jesus said: Do not lie, and do not practice what you hate, for everything is in the plain sight of Heaven. For there is nothing concealed that will not become manifest, and there is nothing covered that will not be exposed.

6.   His disciples asked him, "How do you want us to fast? And how shall we pray? And how shall we give alms? And what kind of diet shall we follow?"

Jesus said, don't lie, and don't do what you hate to do, for all things are revealed before the truth. For there is nothing hidden which shall not be revealed.

No matter what you do on the outside your true nature will be revealed in time. Following codes, practices and rituals will not change who you are. Following such liturgies and rituals are simply lies if you hate doing them.

Luke 11:1 He was praying in a certain place, and after he had finished, one of his disciples said to him, Lord, teach us to pray, as John taught his disciples.

7. Jesus said: Blessed is the lion that the man will eat, for the lion will become the man. Cursed is the man that the lion shall eat, and still the lion will become man.

This saying is a difficult one to understand. A lion was a symbol of many things at this time, ranging from royalty to evil. A lion is also the symbol of God. At one time the lion represented uncontrolled passion. The saying may be interpreted as, "If a lion, the most royal of beasts, were to eat a man, it would be elevated by the nature of the man, but if a man eats a lion (in whatever symbolic capacity), he would be less than what he was.

Mathew 26:23-30 He who dipped his hand with me in the dish, the same will betray me. The Son of Man goes, even as it is written of him, but woe to that man through whom the Son of Man is betrayed! It would be better for that man if he had not been born. Judas, who betrayed him, answered, "It isn't me, is it, Rabbi?" He said to him, You said it. As they were eating, Jesus took bread, gave thanks for it, and broke it. He gave to the disciples, and said, Take, eat; this is my body. He took the cup, gave thanks, and gave to them, saying: All of you drink it, for this is my blood of the new covenant, which is poured out for many for the remission of sins. But I tell you that I will not drink of this fruit of the vine from now on, until that day when I drink it anew with you in my Father's Kingdom. When they had sung a hymn, they went out to the Mount of Olives.

8. And he said: The Kingdom of Heaven is like a wise fisherman who casts his net into the sea. He drew it up from the sea (a net) full of small fish. Among them he found a fine large fish. That wise fisherman threw all the small fish back into the sea and chose the large fish without hesitation.

Whoever has ears to hear, let him hear!

There will be many variations on this theme in the remaining sayings. Many of this saying will be easier to understand if one substitutes the words "kingdom of heaven" or "kingdom" with the words ""the enlightened person" or "the Gnostic". The fine, fatter, or larger of the various prizes represents the knowledge or the gnosis.

The enlightened person is like a wise fisherman who casts his net into the sea (life). He drew up from the sea (life) a net full of small fish (useless things) but there was one fish that was fine (there was the gnosis). He threw everything back and kept that one useful thing.

Matthew 13:47-48 Again, the kingdom of heaven is like a net that was thrown into the sea and caught fish of every kind; when it was full, they drew it ashore, sat down, and put the good into baskets but threw out the bad.

9. Jesus said: Now, the sower came forth. He filled his hand and threw (the seeds). Some fell upon the road and the birds came and gathered them up. Others fell on the stone and they did not take deep enough roots in the soil, and so did not

produce grain. Others fell among the thorns and they choked the seed, and the worm ate them. Others fell upon the good earth and it produced good fruit up toward the sky, it bore 60 fold and 120 fold.

The teaching and the truth is spread over the world. Some will understand the teachings. Some will not. Those who do understand will have levels of understanding depending on the time and effort spent cultivating a deeper gnosis.

Matthew 13:3-8 And he told them many things in parables, saying: Listen! A sower went out to sow. And as he sowed, some seeds fell on the path, and the birds came and ate them up. Other seeds fell on rocky ground, where they did not have much soil, and they sprang up quickly, since they had no depth of soil. But when the sun rose, they were scorched; and since they had no root, they withered away. Other seeds fell among thorns, and the thorns grew up and choked them. Other seeds fell on good soil and brought forth grain, some a hundred fold, some sixty, some thirty.

Mark 4:2-9 And he taught them many things in parables, and in his teaching he said to them: Behold! A sower went out to sow. And as he sowed, some seed fell along the path, and the birds came and devoured it. Other seed fell on rocky ground, where it had not much soil, and immediately it sprang up, since it had no depth of soil; and when the sun rose it was scorched, and since it had no root it withered away. Other seed fell among thorns and the thorns grew up and choked it, and it yielded no grain. And other seeds fell into good soil and brought forth grain, growing up and increasing and yielding thirty fold and sixty fold and a hundred fold. And he said, He who has ears to hear, let him hear.

Luke 8:4-8 And when a great crowd came together and people from town after town came to him, he said in a parable: A sower went out to sow his seed; and as he sowed, some fell along the path, and was trodden under foot, and the birds of the air devoured it. And some fell on the rock; and as it grew up, it withered away, because it had no moisture. And some fell among thorns; and the thorns grew with it and choked it. And some fell into good soil and grew, and yielded a hundred fold. As he said this, he called out, He who has ears to hear, let him hear.

10. Jesus said: I have cast fire upon the world, and as you see, I guard it until it is ablaze.

In Gnostic literature a fire is symbolic of the knowledge.

Luke 12:49 I came to bring fire to the earth, and how I wish it were already kindled.

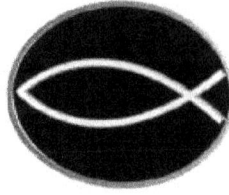

11. Jesus said: This sky will pass away, and the one above it will pass away. The dead are not alive, and the living will not die. In the days when you consumed what is dead, you made it alive. When you come into the Light, what will you do? On the day when you were united (one), you became separated (two). When you have become separated (two), what will you do?

There are, according to Paul, three heavens. The third heaven is the throne of God, called in Gnostic writings "The Fullness" or the Pleroma. All other things will pass away.

*2 Corithians 12:2 I know a man in Christ who fourteen years ago was caught up to the **third heaven**. Whether it was in the body or out of the body I do not know – God knows.*

You can eat that which is dead and it gives you life. As it is spiritually, you can eat the living knowledge and you who are dead will be made alive, but if you are not whole and one with the truth what will you do? Gnosticism preaches unity and wholeness of the person. The parable is asking, "What will you do if you are not whole?"

Matthew 24:35 Heaven and earth will pass away, but my words will not pass away.

12. The Disciples said to Jesus: We know that you will go away from us. Who is it that will be our teacher?

Jesus said to them: Wherever you are (in the place that you have come), you will go to James the Righteous, for whose sake Heaven and Earth were made (came into being).

James was the first leader of the Church in Jerusalem, which was the mother church of Christianity in the first years of the faith. For more information about the theology of James see, "The Didache: The Teaching of the Twelve Apostles: A Different Faith - A Different Salvation."

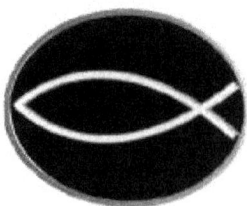

13. Jesus said to his Disciples: Compare me to others, and tell me who I am like. Simon Peter said to him: You are like a righteous messenger (angel) of God. Matthew said to him: You are like a (wise) philosopher (of the heart). Thomas said to him: Teacher, my mouth is not capable of saying who you are like!

Jesus said: I'm not your teacher, now that you have drunk; you have become intoxicated from the bubbling spring that I have tended (measured out). And he took him, and withdrew and spoke three words to him: ahyh ashr ahyh (I am who I am).

Now when Thomas returned to his comrades, they inquired of him: What did Jesus say to you? Thomas said to them: If I tell you even one of the words which he spoke to me, you will take up stones and throw them at me, and fire will come from the stones to consume you.

When Moses asked God for his name (Exodus 3:14) God replied in Exodus 3:12, " *Ehyeh asher ehyeh"*, literally translates as "I Will Be What I Will Be", with attendant theological and mystical implications in Jewish tradition. However, in most English Bibles, this phrase is rendered as *I am that I am."*

Mark 8:27-30 Jesus went on with his disciples to the villages of Caesarea Philippi; and on the way he asked his disciples, Who do people say that I am? And they answered him, John the Baptist; and others, Elijah; and still others, one of the prophets. He asked them, But who do you say that I am? Peter answered him, You are the Messiah. And he sternly ordered them not to tell anyone about him.

14. Jesus said to them: If you fast, you will give rise to transgression (sin) for yourselves. And if you pray, you will be condemned. And if you give alms, you will cause harm (evil) to your spirits. And when you go into the countryside, if they take you in (receive you) then eat what they set before you and heal the sick among them. For what goes into your mouth will not defile you, but rather what comes out of your mouth, that is what will defile you.

What is outside counts little. What is inside counts much. If you do what you hate doing, even if it is "religious" you will harbor resentment and ill thoughts. Do what is in your spirit to do. Do not stress what is done on the outside but rather what comes from the inside. The command to eat whatever is set before you is evidence that the gospel was being propagated to the Gentiles.

Luke 10:8-9 Whenever you enter a town and its people welcome you, eat what is set before you; Cure the sick who are there, and say to them, The kingdom of God has come near to you.

Mark 7:15 There is nothing outside a person that by going in can defile, but the things that come out are what defile.

Matthew 15:11 It is not what goes into the mouth that defiles a man, but what comes out of the mouth, this defiles a man.

Romans 14:14 I know and am persuaded in the Lord Jesus that nothing is unclean in itself; but it is unclean for any one who thinks it unclean.

15. Jesus said: When you see him who was not born of woman, bow yourselves down upon your faces and worship him for he is your Father.

Even Jesus was born of a woman, but more importantly, the

Demiurge was born of Sophia, but the Supreme God was born of himself. It is he whom we should worship.

It bears saying again that one does not need to believe in the actual existence of these beings, but only in the metaphor that is conveyed by the myth.

Galatians 4:3-5 Even so we, when we were children, were in bondage under the elements of the world: But when the fullness of the time was come, God sent forth his Son, made of a woman, made under the law, To redeem them that were under the law, that we might receive the adoption of sons.

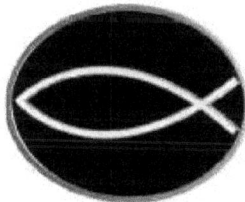

16. **Jesus said: People think perhaps I have come to spread peace upon the world. They do not know that I have come to cast dissention (conflict) upon the earth; fire, sword, war. For there will be five in a house. Three will be against two and**

two against three, the father against the son and the son against the father. And they will as one (as a single unit, they will stand alone).

There will always be enmity between those who are religious and those who are spiritual, even more so if they are awakened. Those who are awakened are those who are a unity unto themselves. This salvation is not a do-it yourself salvation. If it were we would not need a messiah. The messiah is the servant sent to lead us out of the fog and show us our error. He leads us to the path of knowledge and righteousness. It is up to us to walk the path. Those who walk the path will become different from others because their perspective will change. The difference in the enlightened person will be hated by the world.

Matthew 10:34-36 Do not think that I have come to bring peace to the earth; I have not come to bring peace, but a sword. For I have come to set a man against his father, and a daughter against her mother, and a daughter-in-law against her mother-in-law; and one's foes will be members of one's own household.

Luke 12:51-53 Do you think that I have come to give peace on earth? No, I tell you, but rather division; for henceforth in one house there will be five divided, three against two and two against three; they will be divided, father against son and son against father, mother against daughter and daughter against her mother, mother-in-law against her daughter-in-law and daughter-in-law against her mother-in-law.

17. Jesus said: I will give to you what eye has not seen, what ear has not heard, what hand has not touched, and what has not occurred to the mind of man.

This saying enforces that fact we need someone outside our own confused mind to give us what we cannot see or conceive. Our own concepts and ways of thinking have led us in circles like a pony tied to a post and chain.

1 Cor 2:9 But, as it is written, What no eye has seen, nor ear heard, nor the human heart conceived, what God has prepared for those who love him.

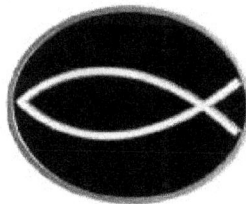

18. The Disciples said to Jesus: Tell us how our end will come. Jesus said: Have you already discovered the beginning

(origin), so that you inquire about the end? Where the beginning (origin) is, there the end will be. Blessed be he who will take his place in the beginning (stand at the origin) for he will know the end, and he will not experience death.

From God we come and to God we return, and remembering our origin is to know our destiny. Jesus told us this again later in Revelation when he proclaimed himself as the Alpha and the Omega.

19. Jesus said: Blessed is he who came into being before he came into being. If you become my Disciples and heed my sayings, these stones will serve you. For there are five trees in paradise for you, which are undisturbed in summer and in winter and their leaves do not fall. Whoever knows them will not experience death.

Jesus came into being with God before he was born of flesh. Moreover, if God created all things in one period of time, as Genesis tells us, then all souls (spirits) existed with him until sent into the bodies of newborns. If we remember where we came from and that we have this divine connection we also fit this description.

Five is the number of grace. It is the grace of God which sends the gnosis.

John 1

King James Version (KJV)

1 In the beginning was the Word, and the Word was with God, and the Word was God.

2 The same was in the beginning with God.

3 All things were made by him; and without him was not any thing made that was made.

4 In him was life; and the life was the light of men.

5 And the light shineth in darkness; and the darkness comprehended it not.

20. The Disciples said to Jesus: Tell us what the Kingdom of Heaven is like. He said to them: It is like a mustard seed, smaller than all other seeds and yet when it falls on the tilled earth, it produces a great plant and becomes shelter for the birds of the sky.

This saying as presented in Luke is an exaggeration, which has no apparent reason. A mustard seed is small but the mustard plant is in no way a tree. It is a vegetable, as Thomas describes it. Luke says the birds nest in the branches. Thomas says the birds shelter beneath it.

When the truth is deposited in the mind and heart it will grow to great dimensions and beneath (within) the truth we will find shelter and rest..

Mark 4:30-32 He also said, With what can we compare the kingdom of God, or what parable will we use for it? It is like a mustard seed, which, when sown upon the ground, is the smallest of all the seeds on earth; yet when it is sown it grows up and becomes the greatest of all shrubs, and puts forth large branches, so that the birds of the air can make nests in its shade.

Matthew 13:31-32 The kingdom of heaven is like a grain of mustard seed which a man took and sowed in his field; it is the smallest of all seeds, but when it has grown it is the greatest of shrubs and becomes a tree, so that the birds of the air come and make nests in its branches.

Luke 13.18-19 He said therefore, What is the kingdom of God like? And to what shall I compare it? It is like a grain of mustard seed which a man took and sowed in his garden; and it grew and became a tree, and the birds of the air made nests in its branches.

21. Mary said to Jesus: Who are your Disciples like? He said: They are like little children who are living in a field that is not theirs. When the owners of the field come, they will say: Let us have our field! It is as if they were naked in front of them (They undress in front of them in order to let them have what is theirs) and they give back the field. Therefore I say, if the owner of the house knows that the thief is coming, he will be alert before he arrives and will not allow him to dig through into the house to carry away his belongings. You, must be on guard and beware of the world (system). Prepare yourself (arm yourself) with great strength or the bandits will find a way to reach you, for the problems you expect will come. Let there be among you a person of understanding (awareness). When the crop ripened, he came quickly with his sickle in his hand to reap. Whoever has ears to hear, let him hear!

Jack Finegan writes: "Here the little children who live in the field are presumably the disciples who live in the world. When they give back the field to its owners they 'take off their clothes before them' which, in the present context, must mean that they strip themselves of their bodies in death, an end, to the Gnostic, eminently desirable (cf. §§236, 357)." (*Hidden Records of the Life of Jesus*, p. 254)

Matthew 24:43 But understand this: if the owner of the house had known in what part of the night the thief was coming, he would have stayed awake and would not have let his house be broken into.

Mark 4:26-29 He also said, The kingdom of God is as if someone would scatter seed on the ground, and would sleep and rise night and day, and the seed would sprout and grow, he does not know how. The earth produces of itself, first the stalk, then the head, then the full grain in the head. But when the grain is ripe, at once he goes in with his sickle, because the harvest has come.

Luke 12:39-40 But know this, that if the householder had known at what hour the thief was coming, he would not have left his house to be broken into. You also must be ready; for the Son of man is coming at an unexpected hour.

22. Jesus saw little children who were being suckled. He said to his Disciples: These little children who are being suckled are like those who enter the Kingdom.

They said to him: Should we become like little children in order to enter the Kingdom?

Jesus said to them: When you make the two one, and you make the inside as the outside and the outside as the inside,

when you make the above as the below, and if you make the male and the female one and the same (united male and female) so that the man will not be masculine (male) and the female be not feminine (female), when you establish an eye in the place of an eye and a hand in the place of a hand and a foot in the place of a foot and an likeness (image) in the place of a likeness (an image), then will you enter the Kingdom.

When there is unity within the person there is wholeness. When there is disunity in the person there is disharmony, confusion and subterfuge. Unity is wholeness and wholeness is simple and childlike. There is no guile.

Luke 18:16 But Jesus called for them and said, Let the little children come to me, and do not stop them; for it is to such as these that the kingdom of God belongs. Truly I tell you, whoever does not receive the kingdom of God as a little child will never enter it.

Mark 9:43-48 If your hand causes you to stumble, cut it off; it is better for you to enter life maimed than to have two hands and to go to hell, to the unquenchable fire. And if your foot causes you to stumble, cut it off; it is better for you to enter life lame than to have two feet and to be thrown into hell. And if your eye causes you to stumble, tear it out; it is better for you to enter the kingdom of God with one eye than to have two eyes and to be thrown into hell, where the worm never dies, and the fire is never quenched.

Matthew 18:3-5 And said, Verily, I say unto you, unless you turn and become like children, you will never enter the kingdom of heaven. Whoever humbles himself like this child, he is the greatest in the kingdom of heaven. Whoever receives one such child in my name receives me;

Matthew 5:29-30 If your right eye causes you to sin, pluck it out and throw it away; it is better that you lose one of your members than that your whole body be thrown into hell. And if your right hand causes you to sin, cut it off and throw it away; it is better that you lose one of your members than that your whole body go into hell.

23. Jesus said: I will choose you, one out of a thousand and two out of ten thousand and they will stand as a single one.

Many are called but few are chosen. This comment about standing as a single one may indicate the Gnostic believed in an undifferentiated and unified existence in heaven.

Matthew 20:16 So the last shall be first, and the first last: for many be called, but few chosen.

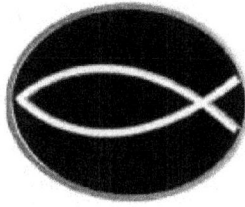

24. **His Disciples said: Show us the place where you are (your place), for it is necessary for us to seek it.**

He said to them: Whoever has ears, let him hear! Within a man of light there is light, and he illumines the entire world. If he does not shine, he is darkness (there is darkness).

The apostles do not yet recognize the light within themselves. By not singling himself out and by using the general term "man" Jesus is telling them they are men of light that should shine.

John13:36 Simon Peter said to him, Lord, where are you going? Jesus answered, Where I am going, you cannot follow me now; but you will follow afterward.

Matthew 6:22-23 The eye is the lamp of the body. So, if your eye is healthy, your whole body will be full of light; but if your eye is unhealthy, your whole body will be full of darkness. If then the light in you is darkness, how great is the darkness!

Luke 11:34-36 Your eye is the lamp of your body; when your eye is sound, your whole body is full of light; but when it is not sound, your body is full of darkness. Therefore be careful lest the light in you be darkness. If then your whole body is full of light, having no part dark, it will be wholly bright, as when a lamp with its rays gives you light.

Early philosophers thought that light was transmitted from the eye and bounced back, allowing the person to sense the world at large. Ancient myths tell of Aphrodite constructing the human eye out of the four elements (earth, wind, fire, and water). The eye was held together by love. She kindled the fire of the soul and used it to project from the eyes so that it would act like a lantern, transmitting the light, thus allowing us to see.

Euclid, (330 BC to 260BC) speculated about the speed of light being instantaneous since you close your eyes, then open them again, even the distant objects appear immediately.

25. Jesus said: Love your friend (Brother) as your soul; protect him as you would the pupil of your own eye.

Although scholars have pointed out that the term "brother" applies only to fellow believers and in this case only fellow Gnostics. I must reject the idea of a narrow scope of compassion and hope it is applied universally.

Romans 12:9-11 Let love be without dissimulation. Abhor that which is evil; cleave to that which is good. Be kindly affectioned one to another with brotherly love; in honour preferring one another; Not slothful in business; fervent in spirit; serving the Lord;

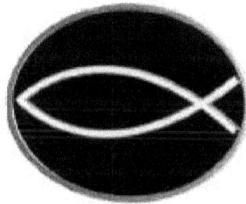

26. Jesus said: You see the speck in your brother's eye but the beam that is in your own eye you do not see. When you remove the beam out of your own eye, then will you see clearly to remove the speck out of your brother's eye.

26.   Jesus said, You see the splinter in your brother's eye, but you don't see the log in your own eye. When you take the log out of your own eye, then you will see well enough to remove the splinter from your brother's eye.

Again we have the term, "brother," indicating the saying applies to a fellow Gnostic. In addressing this it can be pointed out that the majority of fault finding and crass judgment comes from inside the church toward its members. In modern times the majority of serious emotional injury to members of a church are inflicted by other members. However, as with the previous verse, it should be applied universally.

Matthew 7:3-5 Why do you see the speck in your neighbor's eye, but do not notice the log in your own eye? Or how can you say to your neighbor, Let me take the speck out of your eye, while the log is in your own eye? You hypocrite, first take the log out of your own eye, and then you will see clearly to take the speck out of your neighbor's eye.

Luke 6:41-42 Why do you see the speck that is in your brother's eye, but do not notice the log that is in your own eye? Or how can you say to your brother, Brother, let me take out the speck that is in your eye, when you yourself do not see the log that is in your own eye? You hypocrite, first take the log out of your own eye, and then you will see clearly to take out the speck that is in your brother's eye.

27. Jesus said: Unless you fast from the world (system), you will not find the Kingdom of God. Unless you keep the Sabbath (entire week) as Sabbath, you will not see the Father.

27. Jesus said: Unless you fast (abstain) from the world, you shall in no way find the Kingdom of God; and unless you observe the Sabbath as a Sabbath, you shall not see the Father.

The Gnostic view is that the world system was put in place by an evil entity for the purpose of distracting us from our spiritual journey. The world system lulls us into a catatonic state so that we forget our origin, our spiritual substance, and our purpose.

Treating every moment as sacred and turning away from attachment we see the truth and receive the gnosis (kingdom).

28. Jesus said: I stood in the midst of the world. In the flesh I appeared to them. I found them all drunk; I found none

thirsty among them. My soul grieved for the sons of men, for they are blind in their hearts and do not see that they came into the world empty they are destined (determined) to leave the world empty. However, now they are drunk. When they have shaken off their wine, then they will repent (change their ways).

28. Jesus said: I took my stand in the midst of the world, and they saw me in the flesh, and I found they were all drunk, and I found none of them were thirsty. And my soul grieved over the souls of men because they are blind in their hearts. They do not see that they came into the world empty and they are determined to leave the world empty. However, now they are drunk. When they have shaken off their wine, then they will change their ways.

Drunk on the distractions the world has to offer, mankind is oblivious to the messiah and his teaching. In time they may become disenchanted with the empty distractions and be open to his truth.

As discussed in the chapter about Gnosticism, many Gnostics do not believe Jesus came in the flesh, since it was thought that if Jesus were actually God then he would not come to the corrupt material realm. Others postulated that Jesus was a vessel of the Holy Spirit, who departed when Jesus was crucified. If Jesus was simply a man who was appointed he would not be God but would be able to endure the corrupt world.

29. Jesus said: If the flesh came into being because of spirit, it is a marvel, but if spirit came into being because of the body, it would be a marvel of marvels. I marvel indeed at how great wealth has taken up residence in this poverty.

The flesh is a vehicle and can become an encumbrance. It is used to pass through this realm, but can hold us back on our journey. The spirit inhabits this realm of spiritual poverty, of which the body is a sponge for the mire.

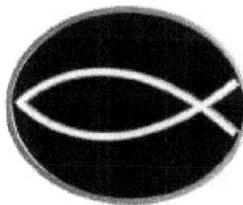

30. Jesus said: Where there are three gods, they are gods

(Where there are three gods they are without god). Where there is only one, I say that I am with him. Lift the stone and there you will find me, Split the wood and there am I.

30. Jesus said: Where three are together they are not without God, and when there is one alone, I say, I am with him.

Other versions read: "Where there are two they are without god but where this is one alone I say I am with him."

The solitary one is a reference to a single person, meaning salvation is a deeply personal transformation accomplished between the individual and God. It is only the person in unity that merits God's presence.

Many believe pages of the manuscript were misplaced and verses 30 and 77 should run together as a single verse.

77. Jesus said: I-Am the Light who is over all things, I-Am the All. From me all came forth and to me all return (The All came from me and the All has come to me). Split wood, there am I. Lift up the stone and there you will find me.

This "I Am" is the same title as God previously described to Moses.

Matthew 18:20 For where two or three are gathered in my name, I am there among them.

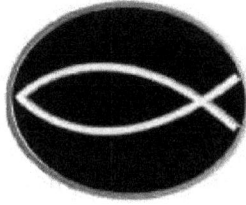

31. Jesus said: No prophet is accepted in his own village, no physician heals those who know him.

31. Jesus said: A prophet is not accepted in his own country; neither can a doctor cure those that know him.

Familiarity breeds contempt, as the saying goes. To have seen Jesus grow up and hear all of the rumors regarding his alleged illegitimate birth brings lack of faith in him. Jesus was rejected in Nazareth.

Mark 6:4 Then Jesus said to them, Prophets are not without honor, except in their hometown, and among their own kin, and in their own house.

Matthew 13:57 And they took offense at him. But Jesus said to them: A prophet is not without honor save in his own country and in his own house.

Luke 4:24 And he said, Truly, I say to you, no prophet is acceptable in his own country.

John 4:43-44 After the two days he departed to Galilee. For Jesus himself testified that a prophet has no honor in his own country.

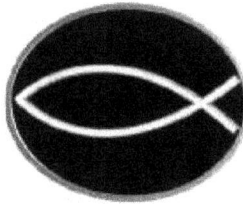

32. Jesus said: A city being built (and established) upon a high mountain and fortified cannot fall nor can it be hidden.

32. Jesus said: A city built on a high hilltop and fortified can neither fall nor be hidden.

The gnosis is not faith as we think of it. It is an experience, which is stronger and cannot be shaken. The enlightened man emits the light of the truth.

Matthew 5:14 You are the light of the world. A city built on a hill cannot be hid.

33. Jesus said: What you will hear in your ear preach from your rooftops. For no one lights a lamp and sets it under a basket nor puts it in a hidden place, but rather it is placed on a lamp stand so that everyone who comes and goes will see its light.

33. Jesus said: What you hear with one ear preach from your rooftops. For no one lights a lamp and sets it under a basket or hides, but rather it is placed on a lamp stand so that everyone who comes and goes will see its light.

As a continuation of saying 32, he urges the disciples to enlighten others with the truth and let their light shine brightly. Of course, this gets Jesus and the majority of the apostles killed.

Matthew 10:27 What I say to you in the dark, tell in the light; and what you hear whispered, proclaim from the housetops.

Luke 8:16 No one after lighting a lamp hides it under a jar, or puts it under a bed, but puts it on a lamp stand, so that those who enter may see the light.

Matthew 5:15 Nor do men light a lamp and put it under a bushel, but on a stand, and it gives light to all in the house.

Mark 4:21 And he said to them, Is a lamp brought in to be put under a bushel, or under a bed, and not on a stand?

Luke 11:33 No one after lighting a lamp puts it in a cellar or under a bushel, but on a stand, that those who enter may see the light.

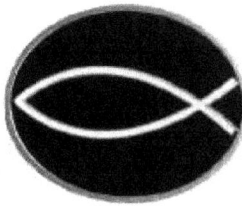

34. Jesus said: If a blind person leads a blind person, both fall into a pit.

Do not follow anyone who has not proven to have the gnosis. If you do you will be led further away from the light.

Matthew 15:14 Let them alone; they are blind guides of the blind. And if one blind person guides another, both will fall into a pit.

Luke 6:39 He also told them a parable: Can a blind man lead a blind man? Will they not both fall into a pit?

35. Jesus said: It is impossible for anyone to enter the house of a strong man to take it by force unless he binds his hands, then he will be able to loot his house.

The Demiurge must be bound with the truth before his processions, his slaves, can be stolen back.

This saying in Mark 3:27 had to do with exorcism. Some scholars do not think this saying was actually attributed to Jesus since it is a violent one.

Matthew 12:29 Or how can one enter a strong man's house and plunder his goods, unless he first binds the strong man? Then indeed he may plunder his house.

Luke 11:21-22 When a strong man, fully armed, guards his own palace, his goods are in peace; but when one stronger than he assails him and overcomes him, he takes away his armor in which he trusted, and divides his spoil.

Mark 3:27 But no one can enter a strong man's house and plunder his property without first tying up the strong man; then indeed the house can be plundered.

36. Jesus said: Do not worry from morning to evening nor from evening to morning about the food that you will eat nor about what clothes you will wear. You are much superior to the Lilies which neither card nor spin. When you have no clothing, what do you wear? Who can add time to your life (increase your stature)? He himself will give to you your garment.

What is here to wear is unimportant. In a short time you will slip out of your body, which was given to you.

Matthew 6:25-31 Therefore I tell you, do not worry about your life, what you will eat or what you will drink, or about your body, what you will wear. Is not life more than food, and the body more than clothing? Look at the birds of the air; they neither sow nor reap nor gather into barns, and yet your heavenly Father feeds them. Are you not of more value than they? And can any of you by worrying add a single hour to your span of life? And why do you worry about clothing? Consider the lilies of the field, how they grow; they neither toil nor spin, yet I tell you, even Solomon in all his glory was not clothed like one of these. But if God so clothes the grass of the field, which is alive today and tomorrow is thrown into the oven, will he not much more clothe you--you of little faith? Therefore do not worry, saying, What will we eat? or What will we drink? or What will we wear?

Luke 12:22-23 And he said to his disciples, Therefore I tell you, do not be anxious about your life, what you shall eat, nor about your body, what you shall put on. For life is more than food, and the body more than clothing.

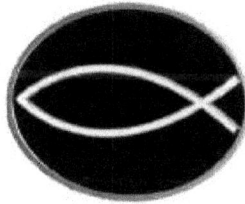

37. His Disciples said: When will you appear to us, and when will we see you?

Jesus said: When you take off your garments without being ashamed, and place your garments under your feet and tread on them as the little children do, then will you see the Son of the Living-One, and you will not be afraid.

37 His disciples said to him, when will you be visible to us, and when shall we be able to see you?

He said, when you strip naked without being ashamed and place your garments under your feet and tread on them as the little children do, then will you see the Son of the Living-One, and you will not be afraid.

The garment refers in metaphor to the body and thus the world or physical realm. When we see the entire truth we will not only be unafraid, but we will be joyous about laying down the body with its weights of the world. In that time we will see him as he is and we will not be afraid.

38. Jesus said: Many times have you yearned to hear these sayings which I speak to you, and you have no one else from whom to hear them. There will be days when you will seek me but you will not find me.

We cannot imagine if we were given time with Jesus that we would waste time. Once he departed we would think of a thousand questions.

Luke 17:22: The days will come when you desire to see one of the days of the Son of Man, and you will not see.

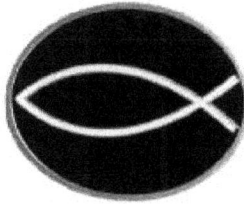

39. Jesus said: The Pharisees and the Scribes have received the keys of knowledge, but they have hidden them. They did not go in, nor did they permit those who wished to enter to do so. However, you be as wise (astute) as serpents and innocent as doves.

39. Jesus said: The Pharisees and the Scribes have stolen the keys of heaven, but they have hidden them. They have entered in, but they did not permit those who wished to enter to do so. However, you be as wise as serpents and innocent as doves.

The religious leaders have been staring at the truth, even scriptures telling of the messiah, but they hid the truth so they could continue in their place of authority and corruption.

Fitzmyer believes this is a combination of two unrelated sayings. His restoration and translation follows with missing or uncertain words in brackets. ['Jesus says, "The Pharisees and the scribes have] re[ceived the keys] of [knowledge and have] hid[den them; neither have they] enter[ed nor permitted those who would] enter.

[But you] bec[ome wi]se a[s the serpents and g]uileless [as the dov]es' (see also Hennecke and Schneemelcher: 1.112-113)." (In Fragments, p. 33)

This is similar to saying #102.

Luke 11:52 Woe to you lawyers! For you have taken away the key of knowledge; you did not enter yourselves, and you hindered those who were entering.

Matthew 10:16 See, I am sending you out like sheep into the midst of wolves; so be wise as serpents and innocent as doves.

Matthew 23.13 But woe unto you, scribes and Pharisees, hypocrites! because you shut the kingdom of heaven against men; for you neither enter yourselves, nor allow those who would enter to go in.

40. Jesus said: A grapevine has been planted outside the (vineyard of the) Father, and since it is not viable (supported) it will be pulled up by its roots and destroyed.

The Demiurge made this material world without the Father's permission outside of the Pleroma (the fullness or Heaven). It is a corrupted cosmos created outside of the perfect place. It will be destroyed in time.

The personal lesson here is obvious. Do not move outside the will, fullness, and grace of God. Listen to the heart, where the gnosis abides and follow its call.

Matthew 15:13 He answered, Every plant that my heavenly Father has not planted will be uprooted.

41. Jesus said: Whoever has (it) in his hand, to him will (more) be given. And whoever does not have, from him will be taken even the small amount which he has.

To some degree, gnosis is a binary state. Once the sleeper is awakened there will be levels of "awakeness" but there will be no more sleep.

Matthew 25:29 For to all those who have, more will be given, and they will have an abundance; but from those who have nothing, even what they have will be taken away.

Luke 19:26 I tell you, that to every one who has will more be given; but from him who has not, even what he has will be taken away.

42. Jesus said: Become passers-by.

It seems the smaller and more direct the saying the more powerful it becomes. To become a passer-by is to have no attachment, either physical or emotional, which would hinder the pilgrim's sojourn through this realm to the higher estate. This is one of the most difficult and ongoing challenge the pilgrim faces.

43. His Disciples said to him: Who are you, that you said these things to us?

Jesus said to them: You do not recognize who I am from what I said to you, but rather you have become like the Jews who either love the tree and hate its fruit, or love the fruit and hate the tree.

The nature of the tree is the nature of the fruit. You cannot hate one and love the other. It is cause and effect and they are inextricably linked. His words and deeds are the fruits which point to his authority.

John 8:25 They said to him, Who are you? Jesus said to them, Why do I speak to you at all?

Matthew 7:16-20 You will know them by their fruits. Are grapes gathered from thorns, or figs from thistles? In the same way, every good tree bears good fruit, but the bad tree bears bad fruit. A good tree cannot bear bad fruit, nor can a bad tree bear good fruit. Every tree that does not bear good fruit is cut down and thrown into the fire. Thus you will know them by their fruits.

44. Jesus said: Whoever blasphemes against the Father, it will be forgiven him. And whoever blasphemes against the Son, it will be forgiven him. Yet whoever blasphemes against the

Holy Spirit, it will not be forgiven him neither on earth nor in heaven.

In some Gnostic systems "Father" or "Father of this world is a title of the Demiurge, while in the Apocryphon of John the supreme God is described as the Holy Spirit. This would make sense of this odd saying. All blasphemes are forgiven except those against the Supreme or True God.

Mark 3:28-29 Truly I tell you, people will be forgiven for their sins and whatever blasphemies they utter; but whoever blasphemes against the Holy Spirit can never have forgiveness, but is guilty of an eternal sin.

Matthew 12:31-32 Therefore I tell you, every sin and blasphemy will be forgiven men, but the blasphemy against the Spirit will not be forgiven. And whoever says a word against the Son of man will be forgiven; but whoever speaks against the Holy Spirit will not be forgiven, either in this age or in the age to come.

Luke 12:10 And every one who speaks a word against the Son of man will be forgiven him; but he who blasphemes against the Holy Spirit will not be forgiven.

45. Jesus said: Grapes are not harvested from thorns, nor are figs gathered from thistles, for they do not give fruit. A good person brings forth goodness out of his storehouse. A bad person brings forth evil out of his evil storehouse which is in his heart, and he speaks evil, for out of the abundance of the heart he brings forth evil.

Evil and good are natural states. The good person does not know he is good. Evil is as innocent as a child, and perniciously selfish. However, true awakening from God allows us to see ourselves as we really are and Gnosis brings about change.

Luke 6:43-45 For no good tree bears bad fruit, nor again does a bad tree bear good fruit; for each tree is known by its own fruit. For figs are not gathered from thorns, nor are grapes picked from a bramble bush. The good man out of the good treasure of his heart produces good, and the evil man out of his evil treasure produces evil; for out of the abundance of the heart his mouth speaks.

46. Jesus said: From Adam until John the Baptist there is none born of women who surpasses John the Baptist, so that his eyes should not be downcast (lowered). Yet I have said that whoever among you becomes like a child will know the

Kingdom, and he will be greater than John.

Jesus expresses appreciation for few people. James, Thomas and John are mentioned with plaudits in the Gospel of Thomas.

Remembering that the Kingdom is another expression of Gnosis, this saying is similar to others, such as the saying exhorting the apostles to become childlike, strip of their clothes and dance on them.

Matthew 11:11 Truly I tell you, among those born of women no one has arisen greater than John the Baptist; yet the least in the kingdom of heaven is greater than he.

Luke 7:28 I tell you, among those born of women none is greater than John; yet he who is least in the kingdom of God is greater than he.

Matthew 18:2-4 He called a child, whom he put among them, and said, Truly I tell you, unless you change and become like children, you will never enter the kingdom of heaven. Whoever becomes humble like this child is the greatest in the kingdom of heaven.

47. Jesus said: It is impossible for a man to mount two horses or to draw two bows, and a servant cannot serve two masters,

otherwise he will honor the one and disrespect the other. **No man drinks vintage wine and immediately desires to drink new wine, and they do not put new wine into old wineskins or they would burst, and they do not put vintage wine into new wineskins or it would spoil (sour). They do not sew an old patch on a new garment because that would cause a split.**

The old and new wine and patches are reversed from the Gospels. Thomas is pointing out the folly of trying to keep the old life when you are reborn. It will end in damage to your spirit.

There is a Zen saying: If you sit, sit; if you stand, stand; do not wobble. There must be a full commitment to the spiritual life in order to reach complete enlightenment. The secular world and the spiritual world do not mix well.

When Peter walked on the water he began to sink when he took his spiritual eyes off Jesus and began to fear. We must stay single-minded. This is wholeness and unity of being. It is not stubbornness.

Matthew 6:24 No one can serve two masters; for a slave will either hate the one and love the other, or be devoted to the one and despise the other. You cannot serve God and wealth.

Matthew 9:16-17 No one sews a piece of cloth, not yet shrunk, on an old cloak, for the patch pulls away from the cloak, and a worse tear is made. Neither is new wine put into old wineskins; otherwise, the skins burst, and the wine is spilled, and the skins are destroyed; but new wine is put into fresh wineskins, and so both are preserved.

Mark 2:21-22 No one sews a piece of unshrunk cloth on an old garment; if he does, the patch tears away from it, the new from the old, and a worse tear is made. And no one puts new wine into old wineskins; if he does, the wine will burst the skins, and the wine is lost, and so are the skins; but new wine is for fresh skins.

Luke 5:36-39 He told them a parable also: No one tears a piece from a new garment and puts it upon an old garment; if he does, he will tear the new, and the piece from the new will not match the old. And no one puts new wine into old wineskins; if he does, the new wine will burst the skins and it will be spilled, and the skins will be destroyed. But new wine must be put into fresh wineskins. And no one after drinking old wine desires new; for he says, "The old is good."

48. Jesus said: If two make peace with each other in this one house, they will say to the mountain: Be moved! and it will be moved.

This saying is similar to saying 106, where two, becoming one, become sons of men and they can move mountains. It is assumed that "making peace" is the same as being one, at least in agreement. Therefore, within this house, which is the body, resides the spirit and the soul. The soul is made up of mind and emotion. If spirit, mind, and heart are made one, there is power beyond imagination. This act is full individuation.

Matthew 18:19 Again, truly I tell you, if two of you agree on earth about anything you ask, it will be done for you by my Father in heaven.

Mark 11:23-24 Truly I tell you, if you say to this mountain, Be taken up and thrown into the sea, and if you do not doubt in your heart, but believe that what you say will come to pass, it will be done for you. So I tell you, whatever you ask for in prayer, believe that you have received it, and it will be yours.

Matthew 17:20 He said to them, Because of your little faith. For truly, I say to you, if you have faith as a grain of mustard seed, you will say to this mountain, Move from here to there, and it will move; and nothing will be impossible to you.

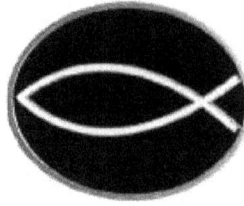

49. Jesus said: Blessed is the solitary and chosen, for you will find the Kingdom. You have come from it, and unto it you will return.

Here, we again find the idea of completeness. The word, "solitary" is unity. Blessed are the complete or unified and selected because you will find the kingdom (or find your way back to the kingdom) because you will remember where you came from and find your way home. This is the knowledge or gnosis we seek.

Matthew 5:1-3 And seeing the multitudes, he went up into a mountain: and when he was set, his disciples came unto him: And he opened his mouth, and taught them, saying, Blessed are the poor in spirit: for theirs is the kingdom of heaven.

John 20:28-30 And Thomas answered and said unto him, My LORD and my God. Jesus saith unto him, Thomas, because thou hast seen me, thou hast believed: blessed are they that have not seen, and yet have believed. And many other signs truly did Jesus in the presence of his disciples, which are not written in this book:

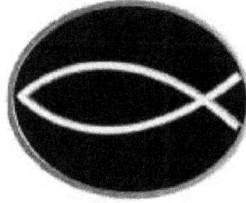

50. Jesus said: If they say to you: From where do you come? Say to them: We have come from the Light, the place where the Light came into existence of its own accord and he stood and appeared in their image. If they say to you: Is it you? (Who are you?), say: We are his Sons and we are the chosen of the Living Father. If they ask you: What is the sign of your Father in you? Say to them: It is movement with rest (peace in the midst of motion or chaos).

Stillness and peace comes from a state of non-attachment. Only here can the ego be at rest and we become an observer instead of a participant caught up in the moment.

Movement is the action of obtaining the realm of fullness. Once there we have rest. Our spirits came from the place of light, and there we return.

51. His Disciples said to him: When will the rest of the dead occur, and when will the New World come? He said to them: That which you look for has already come, but you do not recognize it.

You do not have to wait for death to obtain rest. You, who are dead, will rest when we are awakened and the awakening is taking place now and has taken place already.

Luke 17: [20] And when he was demanded of the Pharisees, when the kingdom of God should come, he answered them and said, The kingdom of God cometh not with observation: [21] Neither shall they say, Lo here! or, lo there! for, behold, the kingdom of God is within you. [22] And he said unto the disciples, The days will come, when ye shall desire to see one of the days of the Son of man, and ye shall not see it. [23] And they shall say to you, See here; or, see there: go not after them, nor follow them.[24] For as the lightning, that lighteneth out of the one part under heaven, shineth unto the other part under heaven; so shall also the Son of man be in his day.[25] But first must he suffer many things, and be rejected of this generation.

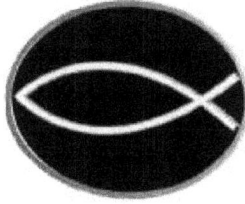

52. His Disciples said to him: Twenty-four prophets preached in Israel, and they all spoke of (in) you. He said to them: You have ignored the Living-One who is in your presence and you have spoken only of the dead.

The 24 referred to are the 24 books of the Hebrew bible. Christ is the fulfillment of all of these. The books are not living, although it is said they contain the living word. Jesus IS the living word, the Logos, and he is there with them. Some had rather read about truth than experience it because that may cause them to change and upset their viewpoints and their life.

John 13: [31] Therefore, when he was gone out, Jesus said, Now is the Son of man glorified, and God is glorified in him.[32] If God be glorified in him, God shall also glorify him in himself, and shall straightway glorify him.[33] Little children, yet a little while I am with you. Ye shall seek me: and as I said unto the Jews,

Whither I go, ye cannot come; so now I say to you.[34] A new commandment I give unto you, That ye love one another; as I have loved you, that ye also love one another.[35] By this shall all men know that ye are my disciples, if ye have love one to another.[36] Simon Peter said unto him, Lord, whither goest thou? Jesus answered him, Whither I go, thou canst not follow me now; but thou shalt follow me afterwards.

53. His Disciples said to him: Is circumcision beneficial or not? He said to them: If it were beneficial, their father would beget them already circumcised from their mother. However, the true spiritual circumcision has become entirely beneficial.

Over and again in Gnostic literature the theme of inner and outer occurs wherein the outer of the physical world is deemed worthless to the spirit. This is one of the issues that brought contention between Gnostics and the other movements claiming orthodoxy. The outward circumcision is useless, but the circumcision of the heart is of great use. Cut away that which is useless and it reveals the truth.

According to a Jewish tradition, a governor of Judea once commented to Rabbi Akiba, 'If he (that is, God) takes such pleasure in circumcision, why then does not a child come circumcised from his mother's womb?'" (Marvin Meyer, The Gospel of Thomas: The Hidden Sayings of Jesus, pp. 90-91)

Jeremiah 4:3-5 For thus saith the LORD to the men of Judah and Jerusalem, Break up your fallow ground, and sow not among thorns. Circumcise yourselves to the LORD, and take away the foreskins of your heart, ye men of Judah and inhabitants of Jerusalem: lest my fury come forth like fire, and burn that none can quench it, because of the evil of your doings. Declare ye in Judah, and publish in Jerusalem; and say, Blow ye the trumpet in the land: cry, gather together, and say, Assemble yourselves, and let us go into the defenced cities.

54. Jesus said: Blessed be the poor, for yours is the Kingdom of the Heaven.

The poor have less of the material world for attachments. Maybe the poor have already learned that this world offers little to stay for.

Often we fall into the trap of thinking that God has blessed those who are wealthy. Wealth, as we see from the parable of the rich young ruler, can be a curse.

Matthew 6:20 Then he looked up at his disciples and said: Blessed are you who are poor, for yours is the kingdom of God.

Luke 6:20 And he lifted up his eyes on his disciples, and said: Blessed are you poor, for yours is the kingdom of God.

Matthew 5:3 Blessed are the poor in spirit, for theirs is the kingdom of heaven.

55. Jesus said: Whoever does not hate his father and his mother will not be able to become my Disciple. And whoever does not hate his brothers and his sisters and does not take up his own cross in my way, will not become worthy of me.

This saying should not be taken literally. There is no room for hate in the way we interpret it. Mother, father, and brother are those in this world following the outward way, attached to the world, including family, and ignoring or numbed to the truth, being that all things placed here in the physical world, including family, are a distraction to the journey. As a matter of fact, drama within families can serve as the greatest distraction. We have seen in other sayings that our true family are those we walk with in the solidarity of the truth.

Luke 14:26-27 If any one comes to me and does not hate his own father and mother and wife and children and brothers and sisters, yes, and even his own life, he cannot be my disciple. Whoever does not bear his own cross and come after me, cannot be my disciple.

John 17:11-21 And now I am no more in the world, but these are in the world, and I come to thee. Holy Father, keep through thine own name those whom thou hast given me, that they may be one, as we are. While I was with them in the world, I kept them in thy name: those that thou gavest me I have kept, and none of them is lost, but the son of perdition; that the scripture might be fulfilled. And now come I to thee; and these things I speak in the world, that they might have my joy fulfilled in themselves. I have given them thy word; and the world hath hated them, because they are not of the world, even as I am not of the world. I pray not that thou shouldest take them out of the world, but that thou shouldest keep them from the evil. They are not of the world, even as I am not of the world. Sanctify them through thy truth: thy word is truth. As thou hast sent me into the world, even so have I also sent them into the world. And for their sakes I sanctify myself, that they also might be sanctified through the truth. Neither pray I for these alone, but for them also which shall believe on me through their word; That they all may be one; as thou, Father, art in me, and I in thee, that they also may be one in us: that the world may believe that thou hast sent me.

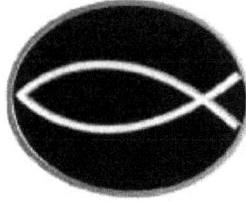

56. Jesus said: Whoever has come to understand the world (system) has found a corpse, and whoever has found a corpse, is superior to the world (of him the system is not worthy).

When you see the world system for what it is, a sham and a trap, you will know its lack of worth and you will know you are better than that.

Luke 9:24 And he said to them all, If any man will come after me, let him deny himself, and take up his cross daily, and follow me.

Hebrews 11:37-40 They were stoned, they were sawn asunder, were tempted, were slain with the sword: they wandered about in sheepskins and goatskins; being destitute, afflicted, tormented; (Of whom the world was not worthy:) they wandered in deserts, and in mountains, and in dens and caves of the earth. And these all, having obtained a good report through faith, received not the promise: God having provided some better thing for us, that they without us should not be made perfect.

57. Jesus said: The Kingdom of the Father is like a person who has good seed. His enemy came by night and sowed a weed among the good seed. The man did not permit them to pull up the weed, he said to them: perhaps you will intend to pull up the weed and you pull up the wheat along with it. But, on the day of harvest the weeds will be very visible and then they will pull them and burn them.

This verse draws us back to the Gnostic belief that the physical realm was put in place by a lower god, an insane angel, who viewed himself as god, and who seeks to entrap men into a continuing worship of him and his creation. In time the differences between his captives and the free enlightened ones will be very clear.

Matthew 13:24-30 He put before them another parable: The kingdom of heaven may be compared to someone who sowed good seed in his field; but while everybody was asleep, an enemy came and sowed weeds among the wheat, and then went away. So when the plants came up and bore grain, then the weeds appeared as well. And the slaves of the householder came and said to him, Master, did you not sow good seed in your field? Where, then, did these weeds come from? He answered, An enemy has done this. The slaves said to him, Then do you want us to go and gather them? But he replied, No; for in gathering the weeds you would uproot the wheat along with them. Let both of them grow together until the harvest; and at harvest time I will tell the reapers, Collect the weeds first and bind them in bundles to be burned, but gather the wheat into my barn.

58. Jesus said: Blessed is the person who has suffered, for he has found life. (Blessed is he who has suffered (labored) to find life and has found life).

The search for truth is a labor. Being truthful and authentic with oneself is suffering. The seeker will find, but only in God's time, since it is he who must reveal himself to us.

Matthew 11:28 Come to me, all you that are weary and are carrying heavy burdens, and I will give you rest.

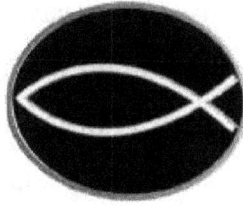

59. Jesus said: Look to the Living-One while you are alive, otherwise, you might die and seek to see him and will be unable to find him.

The Living-One refers to Jesus after the resurrection. Reach for God while you are still awake from the initial jolt of the enlightened truth because you may fall back to sleep if you wait too long, as unused epiphanies tend to fade away.

John 7:34 You will search for me, but you will not find me; and where I am, you cannot come.

John 13:33 Little children, I am with you only a little longer. You will look for me; and as I said to the Jews so now I say to you, Where I am going, you cannot come.

60. They (Jesus and the apostles) saw a Samaritan carrying a lamb, on Jesus' way to Judea. Jesus said to them: Why does

he take the lamb with him? They said to him: So that he may kill it and eat it. He said to them: While it is alive he will not eat it, but only after he kills it and it becomes a corpse. They said: How could he do otherwise? He said to them: Look for a place of rest for yourselves, otherwise, you might become corpses and be eaten.

The codex is damaged here and the verse is unclear. It is reconstructed as a best-guess, based on content and context available.

The place of rest always refers to our realization of the truth and place or state of enlightenment. Seeing the truth makes us alive. While we are alive the world can no longer keep us or destroy us. We must seek the Gnosis and rest that comes with it before we are turned into the world and are trapped.

61. Jesus said: Two will rest on a bed and one will die and the other will live. Salome said: Who are you, man? As if sent by someone, you laid upon my bed and you ate from my table. Jesus said to her: I-Am he who is from that which is whole (the undivided). I have been given the things of my Father. Salome said: I'm your Disciple. Jesus said to her: Thus, I say that whenever someone is one (undivided)

he will be filled with light, yet whenever he is divided he will be filled with darkness.

In those days they reclined on a couch near the table to eat. There were certain positions at the table reserved for those who were invited. Jesus reclined to eat. His actions beg a challenge, as if he is baiting her to speak. Then he pours this simply, yet complex truth out like food before her. You must be whole or you will be in darkness and filled with darkness.

Luke 17:34 I tell you, on that night there will be two in one bed; one will be taken and the other left.

62. Jesus said: I tell my mysteries to those who are worthy of my mysteries. Do not let your right hand know what your left hand is doing.

The right hand is the symbol of rightness, power, and good. The word for "left" is where we get the words, "sinister" and "gauche". I have told you things because you have become righteous (sacred). Do not give what is sacred to those who are not.

Mark 4:11 And he said to them, To you has been given the secret of the kingdom of God, but for those outside, everything comes in parables.

Matthew 6:3 But when you give alms, do not let your left hand know what your right hand is doing.

Luke 8:10 He said, To you it has been given to know the secrets of the kingdom of God; but for others they are in parables, so that seeing they may not see, and hearing they may not understand.

Matthew 13:10-11 Then the disciples came and said to him, Why do you speak to them in parables? And he answered them, To you it has been given to know the secrets of the kingdom of heaven, but to them it has not been given.

63. Jesus said: There was a wealthy person who had much money, and he said: I will use my money so that I may sow and reap and replant, to fill my storehouses with grain so that I lack nothing. This was his intention (is what he thought in his heart) but that same night he died. Whoever has ears, let him hear!

A rich man from the city has plans to invest his money, but he should have taken care of the more important thing first.

Luke 12:21 Then he told them a parable: The land of a rich man produced abundantly. And he thought to himself, What should I do, for I have no place to store my crops? Then he said, I will do this: I will pull down my barns and build larger ones, and there I will store all my grain and my goods. And I will say to my soul, Soul, you have ample goods laid up for many years; relax, eat, drink, be merry. But God said to him, You fool! This very night your life is being demanded of you. And the things you have prepared, whose will they be? So it is with those who store up treasures for themselves but are not rich toward God.

64. Jesus said: A person had houseguests, and when he had prepared the banquet in their honor he sent his servant to invite the guests. He went to the first, he said to him: My master invites you. He replied: I have to do business with some merchants. They are coming to see me this evening. I will go to place my orders with them. I ask to be excused from the banquet. He went to another, he said to him: My master has invited you. He replied to him: I have just bought a house and they require me for a day. I will have no spare time. He came to another, he said to him: My master invites you. He replied to him: My friend is getting married and I must arrange a banquet for him. I will not be able to come. I ask to be excused from the banquet. He went to another, he

said to him: My master invites you. He replied to him: I have bought a farm. I go to receive the rent. I will not be able to come. I ask to be excused. The servant returned, he said to his master: Those whom you have invited to the banquet have excused themselves. The master said to his servant: Go out to the roads, bring those whom you find so that they may feast. And he said: Businessmen and merchants will not enter the places of my Father.

Jesus is the Bridegroom. It is customary to come to the reception and receive a gift, but few came and took the gift that was offered. Those who are too busy will be overlooked in place of those who are less rooted in the world and thus have more time for spiritual matters.

Luke 14:16-24 Then Jesus said to him:, Someone gave a great dinner and invited many. At the time for the dinner he sent his slave to say to those who had been invited, Come; for everything is ready now. But they all alike began to make excuses. The first said to him, I have bought a piece of land, and I must go out and see it; please accept my regrets. Another said, I have bought five yoke of oxen, and I am going to try them out; please accept my regrets. Another said, I have just been married, and therefore I cannot come. So the slave returned and reported this to his master. Then the owner of the house became angry and said to his slave, Go out at once into the streets and lanes of the town and bring in the poor, the crippled, the blind, and the lame. And the slave said, Sir, what you ordered has been done, and there is still room. Then the master said to the slave, Go out into the roads and lanes, and compel people to come in, so that my house may be filled. For I tell you, none of those who were invited will taste my dinner.

Matthew 19:23 Then Jesus said to his disciples, Truly I tell you, it will be hard for a rich person to enter the kingdom of heaven.

Matthew 22:1-14 And Jesus answered and spake unto them again by parables, and said, The kingdom of heaven is like unto a certain king, which made a marriage for his son, and sent his servants to call those who were invited to the marriage feast; but they would not come. Again he sent other servants, saying, Tell those who are invited, Behold, I have made ready my dinner, my oxen and my fat calves are killed, and everything is ready; come to the marriage feast. But they made light of it and went off, one to his farm, another to his business, while the rest seized his servants, treated them shamefully, and killed them. The king was angry, and he sent his troops and destroyed those murderers and burned their city. Then he said to his servants, The wedding is ready, but those invited were not worthy. Go therefore to the thoroughfares, and invite to the marriage feast as many as you find. And those servants went out into the streets and gathered all whom they found, both bad and good; so the wedding hall was filled with guests. But when the king came in to look at the guests, he saw there a man who had no wedding garment; and he said to him, Friend, how did you get in here without a wedding garment? And he was speechless. Then the king said to the attendants, Bind him hand and foot, and cast him into the outer darkness; there men will weep and gnash their teeth. For many are called, but few are chosen.

65. He said: A kind person who owned a vineyard leased it to tenants so that they would work it and he would receive the fruit from them. He sent his servant so that the tenants would give to him the fruit of the vineyard. They seized his servant and beat him nearly to death. The servant went, he told his master what had happened. His master said: Perhaps they did not recognize him. So, he sent another servant. The tenants beat him also. Then the owner sent his son. He said: Perhaps they will respect my son. Since the tenants knew that he was the heir to the vineyard, they seized him and killed him. Whoever has ears, let him hear!

Judaism accepts the fact that there have been multiple messiahs. Kind David was considered one, but when God's servant was sent to take the people the truth and introduce them to the true God they crucified him because they did not want to give up the fruits of the world.

Matthew 21:33-39 Listen to another parable. There was a landowner who planted a vineyard, put a fence around it, dug a wine press in it, and built a watchtower. Then he leased it to tenants and went to another country. When the harvest time had come, he sent his slaves to the tenants to collect his produce. But the tenants seized his slaves and beat one, killed another, and stoned another. Again he sent other slaves, more than the first; and they treated them in the same way. Finally he sent his son to them, saying, They will respect my son. But when the tenants saw the son, they said to themselves, This is the heir; come, let us kill him and get his inheritance. So they seized him, threw him out of the vineyard, and killed him.

Mark 12:1-9 And he began to speak to them in parables. A man planted a vineyard, and set a hedge around it, and dug a pit for the wine press, and built a tower, and let it out to tenants, and went into another country. When the time came, he sent a servant to the tenants, to get from them some of the fruit of the vineyard. And they took him and beat him, and sent him away empty-handed. Again he sent to them another servant, and they wounded him in the head, and treated him shamefully. And he sent another, and him they killed; and so with many others, some they beat and some they killed. He had still one other, a beloved son; finally he sent him to them, saying, They will respect my son. But those tenants said to one another, This is the heir; come, let us kill him, and the inheritance will be ours. And they took him and killed him, and cast him out of the vineyard. What will the owner of the vineyard do? He will come and destroy the tenants, and give the vineyard to others.

Luke 20:9-16 And he began to tell the people this parable: A man planted a vineyard, and let it out to tenants, and went into another country for a long while. When the time came, he sent a servant to the tenants, that they should give him some of the fruit of the vineyard; but the tenants beat him, and sent him away empty-handed. And he sent another servant; him also they beat and treated shamefully, and sent him away empty-handed. And he sent yet a third; this one they wounded and cast out. 13 Then the owner of the vineyard said, What shall I do? I will send my beloved son; it may be they will respect him. 14 But when the tenants saw him, they said to themselves, This is the heir; let us kill him, that the inheritance may be ours. 15 And they cast him out of the vineyard and killed him. What then will the owner of the vineyard do to them? 16 He will come and destroy those tenants, and give the vineyard to others. When they heard this, they said, God forbid!

66. Jesus said: Show me the stone which the builders have rejected. It is that one that is the cornerstone (keystone).

The truth is contrary to what is considered normal or good. It is therefore discarded by most.

Matthew 21:42 Jesus said to them, Have you never read in the scriptures: The very stone which the builders rejected has become the head of the corner; this was the Lord's doing, and it is marvelous in our eyes?

Mark 12:10-11 Have you not read this scripture: The very stone which the builders rejected has become the head of the corner; this was the Lord's doing, and it is marvelous in our eyes?

Luke 20:17 But he looked at them and said, What then does this text mean: The stone that the builders rejected has become the cornerstone?

67. Jesus said: Those who know everything but themselves, lack everything. (Whoever knows the all and still feels a personal lacking, he is completely deficient).

Self-knowledge is a very important tenant in the Gospel of Thomas. If we do not know ourselves and examine ourselves how can we know that we lack something?

There is a theme in Gnosticism of a "homesickness." As my grandfather has been quoted, "I am homesick for a place I have never been." Yet, maybe we have been there and do not fully remember. The place still calls to us in our deeper spirit.

Jeremiah 17:5- 10 Thus saith the LORD; Cursed be the man that trusteth in man, and maketh flesh his arm, and whose heart departeth from the LORD. For he shall be like the heath in the desert, and shall not see when good cometh; but shall inhabit the parched places in the wilderness, in a salt land and not inhabited. Blessed is the man that trusteth in the LORD, and whose hope the LORD is. For he shall be as a tree planted by the waters, and that spreadeth out her roots by the river, and shall not see when heat cometh, but her leaf shall be green; and shall not be careful in the year of drought, neither shall cease from yielding fruit. The heart is deceitful above all things, and desperately wicked: who can know it? I the LORD search the heart, I try the reins, even to give every man according to his ways, and according to the fruit of his doings.

68. Jesus said: Blessed are you when you are hated and persecuted, but they themselves will find no reason why you have been persecuted.

The world, its maker, and those trapped by the system and illusion are in enmity with the real God and those seeking him. They would rather destroy the seeker than to free him.

Matthew 5:11 Blessed are you when people revile you and persecute you and utter all kinds of evil against you falsely on my account.

Luke 6:22 Blessed are you when men hate you, and when they exclude you and revile you, and cast out your name as evil, on account of the Son of man!

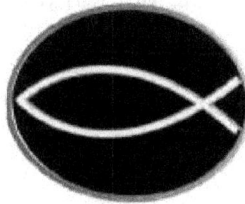

69. Jesus said: Blessed are those who have been persecuted in their heart these are they who have come to know the Father in truth. Jesus said: Blessed are the hungry, for the stomach of him who desires to be filled will be filled.

Rumi said: I am waiting for the guest. It is the longing that does the work.

Matthew 5:8 Blessed are the pure in heart, for they will see God.

Luke 6:21 Blessed are you who are hungry now, for you will be filled.

70. Jesus said: If you bring forth what is within you, it will save you. If you do not have it within you to bring forth, that which you lack will destroy you.

Out of all mysteries written within the Gospel of Thomas, this verse is the most profound. It is perhaps the simplest, yet the most difficult to fulfill. If the person has within the soul what is needed to be whole, integrated, and complete, if these things are brought forth it will save them. If the truth of the Supreme God is within them it will save them. If the spirit and soul, the male and female parts can be made one again they will be saved (made whole). If the person does not have these things inside them they will be lost in spiritual blindness and coma forever.

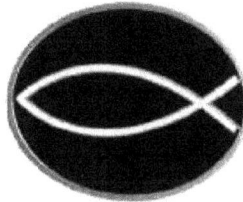

71. Jesus said: I will destroy this house, and no one will be able to build it again.

The body was considered a vessel or house entrapping the soul. To destroy it was to free the soul. It is upon this idea that the Gospel of Judas hangs.

Mark 14:58 We heard him say, I will destroy this temple that is made with hands, and in three days I will build another, not made with hands.

72. A person said to him: Tell my brothers to divide the possessions of my father with me. He said to him: Oh man, who made me a divider? He turned to his Disciples, he said to them: I'm not a divider, am I?

Jesus does not care for the laws of man but instead is working to teach the laws of God. These trivial material matters do not matter. He communicates this almost as a joke. He has already said he has come to divide and set ablaze. He seems to be mocking the man for caring about such minor issues and causing division when Jesus is about to divide the world.

Luke 12:13-15 Someone in the crowd said to him, Teacher, tell my brother to divide the family inheritance with me. But he said to him, Friend, who set me to be a judge or arbitrator over you? And he said to them, Take care! Be on your guard against all kinds of greed; for one's life does not consist in the abundance of possessions.

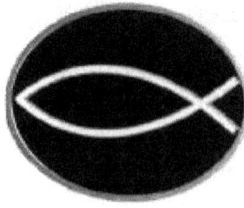

73. Jesus said: The harvest is indeed plentiful, but the workers are few. Ask the Lord to send workers for the harvest.

Although time is running out and the fire of Gnosis has been set, even with eternal life at stake, there are few willing to come forward, leave their old ways, and work for the kingdom.

Matthew 9:37-38 Then he said to his disciples, The harvest is plentiful, but the laborers are few; therefore ask the Lord of the harvest to send out laborers into his harvest.

74. He said: Lord, there are many around the well, yet there is nothing in the well. How is it that many are around the well and no one goes into it?

There is no water around the well, and nothing of value left in it. But if one goes down the metaphorical well and digs he will find running (living) water. Many talked about what Jesus was saying. Few dug in to apply it.

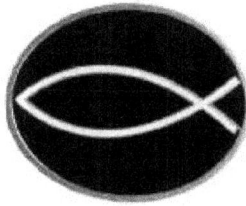

75. Jesus said: There are many standing at the door, but only those who are alone are the ones who will enter into the Bridal Chamber.

The many who stood before the door are probably the foolish virgins of Matthew 25:1-13. The foolish had no oil for their lamps, and therefore no light, a symbol of gnosis. Only the wise virgins enter.

The Bridal Chamber is referred to in the Gospel of Philip as a sacrament. In the chamber the male and female are united. The person is made whole as spirit and soul come together. The splitting apart and cleaving of wholeness is symbolized in the story of Adam and Eve, according to the Gnostics. When Eve came out of Adam it symbolized the separation or division within a single person of their soul (mind and emotions) away from their spirit (that part of us imparted by the divine. Keeping with the theory of wholeness and Jung's individuation these parts must once again be merged to form a complete person, capable of accessing their true divine nature.

Matthew 25:1-8 Then shall the kingdom of heaven be likened unto ten virgins, which took their lamps, and went forth to meet the bridegroom. And five of them were wise, and five were foolish. They that were foolish took their lamps, and took no oil with them: But the wise took oil in their vessels with their lamps. While the bridegroom tarried, they all slumbered and slept. And at midnight there was a cry made, Behold, the bridegroom cometh; go ye out to meet him. Then all those virgins arose, and trimmed their lamps. And the foolish said unto the wise, Give us of your oil; for our lamps are gone out.

76. Jesus said: The Kingdom of the Father is like a rich merchant who found a pearl. The merchant was prudent. He sold his fortune and bought the one pearl for himself. You also, seek for his treasure which does not fail, which endures where no moth (rust) can come near to eat it nor worm to devour it.

In ancient days the pearl was one of the most precious of "stones". The creation of a pearl only comes through pain, for the pearl is the tear of the oyster.

Matthew 13:45-46 Again, the kingdom of heaven is like a merchant in search of fine pearls; on finding one pearl of great value, he went and sold all that he had and bought it.

Matthew 6:19-20 Do not store up for yourselves treasures on earth, where moth and rust consume and where thieves break in and steal; but store up for yourselves treasures in heaven, where neither moth nor rust consumes and where thieves do not break in and steal.

77. Jesus said: I-Am the Light who is over all things, I-Am the All. From me all came forth and to me all return (The All came from me and the All has come to me). Split wood, there am I. Lift up the stone and there you will find me.

Acts of Peter, Chapter 39: You are The All, and The All is within you, and (therefore) you exist! And there is nothing else that exists, except you alone!' *Colossians 3:* 11: 'Christ is all and in all.'"

Note:
Many scholars believe the order of verses 30 and 77 were misplaced and these two verses should be connected as one verse.

30. Jesus said: Where there are three gods, they are gods (Where there are three gods they are without god). Where there is only one, I say that I am with him. Lift the stone and there you will find me, Split the wood and there am I.

God is everywhere and in every mundane object and task of life he can be found if you look for him.

John 8:12 Again Jesus spoke to them, saying, I am the light of the world. Whoever follows me will never walk in darkness but will have the light of life.

John 1:3 All things came into being through him, and without him not one thing came into being.

78. Jesus said: Why did you come out to the wilderness; to see a reed shaken by the wind? And to see a person dressed in fine (soft – plush) garments like your rulers and your dignitaries? They are clothed in plush garments, and they are not able to recognize (understand) the truth.

Matthew 11:7-9 As they went away, Jesus began to speak to the crowds about John: What did you go out into the wilderness to look at? A reed shaken by the wind? What then did you go out to see? Someone dressed in soft robes? Look, those who wear soft robes are in royal palaces. What then did you go out to see? A prophet? Yes, I tell you, and more than a prophet.

79. A woman from the multitude said to him: Blessed is the womb which bore you, and the breasts which nursed you! He said to her: Blessed are those who have heard the word (meaning) of the Father and have truly kept it. For there will be days when you will say: Blessed be the womb which has not conceived and the breasts which have not nursed.

Motherhood is a blessed thing but the state of motherhood binds both mother and child together to the material world, making escape all the more difficult.

Luke 11:27-28 While he was saying this, a woman in the crowd raised her voice and said to him, Blessed is the womb that bore you and the breasts that nursed you! But he said, Blessed rather are those who hear the word of God and obey it!

Luke 23:29 For the days are surely coming when they will say, Blessed are the barren, and the wombs that never bore, and the breasts that never nursed.

80. Jesus said: Whoever has come to understand (recognize) the world (world system) has found the body (corpse), and whoever has found the body (corpse), of him the world (world system) is not worthy.

If you understand the world is dead spiritually you are already above the world.

Hebrews 11:37-40 They were stoned, they were sawn asunder, were tempted, were slain with the sword: they wandered about in sheepskins and goatskins; being destitute, afflicted, tormented; (Of whom the world was not worthy:) they wandered in deserts, and in mountains, and in dens and caves of the earth. And these all, having obtained a good report through faith, received not the promise: God having provided some better thing for us, that they without us should not be made perfect.

81. Jesus said: Whoever has become rich should reign, and let whoever has power renounce it.

This paradoxical saying refers to the richness of the spiritual life as opposed to the power wielded in the material life.

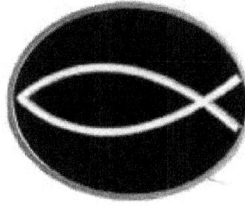

82. Jesus said: Whoever is close to me is close to the fire, and whoever is far from me is far from the Kingdom.

The fire is the gnosis that Jesus came to cast on the earth referred to in sayings 9 and 16. Gnosis leads to the kingdom. The journey is not an easy one. Standing close to the fire is uncomfortable.

John 14:6-9 Jesus saith unto him, I am the way, the truth, and the life: no man cometh unto the Father, but by me. If ye had known me, ye should have known my Father also: and from henceforth ye know him, and have seen him. Philip saith unto him, Lord, show us the Father, and it sufficeth us. Jesus saith unto him, Have I been so long time with you, and yet hast thou not known me, Philip? he that hath seen me hath seen the Father;

83. Jesus said: Images are visible to man but the light which is within them is hidden. The light of the father will be revealed, but he (his image) is hidden in the light.

Sophia hid the light of God in the creation of the Demiurge to bring forth the form with spirit called man. Yet, when one looks into the pure light only the light can be seen. The source is hidden behind the light.

84. Jesus said: When you see your reflection, you rejoice. Yet when you perceive your images which have come into being before you, which neither die nor can be seen, how will you bear the greatness of it?

When we see Christ we will see that we are like him. We have been changed to be like him. Christ is the light of the world. Gnosis is fire and fire is light and we shall be alight.

85. Jesus said: Adam came into existence from a great power and a great wealth, and yet he was not worthy of you. For if he had been worthy, he would not have tasted death.
Yaldabaoth stole great power from his mother, Sophia and created man, very imperfectly and without a spirit. Sophia took pity and gave man a spirit. Yet Adam never received full Gnosis because he did not know Jesus or His wisdom.

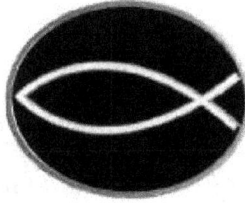

86. Jesus said: The foxes have their dens and the birds have their nests, yet the Son of Man has no place to lay his head for rest.

Jesus has assumed the highest level of material life, that of a pilgrim. He had renounced the material world and has given up even his bedroll.

Matthew 8:20 And Jesus said to him, Foxes have holes, and birds of the air have nests; but the Son of Man has nowhere to lay his head.

87. Jesus said: Wretched is the body which depends upon another body, and wretched is the soul which depends on these two (upon their being together).

Jean Doresse writes: "No doubt this is to be explained by *Luke* IX, 57-60 and *Matt.* VIII, 21-2: 'Let the dead bury the dead.' In this case, 'the body which depends on a body' is a living person who, through care for earthly obligations, wishes to bury his dead person. 'The soul which depends on these two' is the soul of such a person, a living body depending on a dead body." (*The Secret Books of the Egyptian Gnostics*, p. 377)

To break all earthly ties we should leave the dead. This includes the physically dead and the spiritually dead.

88. Jesus said: The messengers and the prophets will come to you, and what they will give you things you already possess. And you will give them what you have, and say among yourselves: When will they come to take (receive) what belongs to them?

The old prophets and messengers are trying to preach to you about things you know more about than they do. You will ask yourself when they will come to understand they do not have the complete truth and when they will seek it.

89. Jesus said: Why do you wash the outside of your cup? Do you not understand (mind) that He who creates the inside is also He who creates the outside?

The Jews were very concerned about keeping the laws. By the time of Jesus there were over 600 laws to be kept, yet if you are so concerned about the law you have no time left for the spirit. This is why Jesus broke everything down to two laws. Love others and love God. Then he said, if you hate doing something, do not do it because your hate will betray you.

Luke 11:39-40 Then the Lord said to him, Now you Pharisees clean the outside of the cup and of the dish, but inside you are full of greed and wickedness. You fools! Did not the one who made the outside make the inside also?

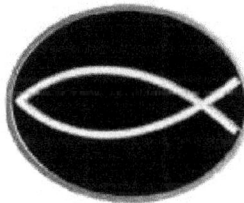

90. Jesus said: Come unto me, for my yoke is comfortable (natural) and my lordship is gentle— and you will find rest for yourselves.

Come under the mastership of Jesus and do as he instructs and all will be well with you.

Matthew 11:28-30 Come to me, all you that are weary and are carrying heavy burdens, and I will give you rest. Take my yoke upon you, and learn from me; for I am gentle and humble in heart, and you will find rest for your souls. For my yoke is easy, and my burden is light.

Acts 15:5-17 But there rose up certain of the sect of the Pharisees which believed, saying, That it was needful to circumcise them, and to command them to keep the law of Moses. And the apostles and elders came together for to consider of this matter. And when there had been much disputing, Peter rose up, and said unto them, Men and brethren, ye know how that a good while ago God made choice among us, that the Gentiles by my mouth should hear the word of the gospel, and believe. And God, which knoweth the hearts, bare them witness, giving them the Holy Ghost, even as he did unto us; And put no difference between us and them, purifying their hearts by faith. Now therefore why tempt ye God, to put a yoke upon the neck of the disciples, which neither our fathers nor we were able to bear? But we believe that through the grace of the LORD Jesus Christ we shall be saved, even as they. Then all the multitude kept silence, and gave audience to Barnabas and Paul, declaring what miracles and wonders God had wrought among the Gentiles by them. And after they had held their peace, James answered, saying, Men and brethren, hearken unto me: Simeon hath declared how God at the first did visit the Gentiles, to take out of them a people for his name. And to this agree the words of the prophets; as it is written, After this I will return, and will build again the tabernacle of David, which is fallen down; and I will build again the ruins thereof, and I will set it up: That the residue of men might seek after the Lord, and all the Gentiles, upon whom my name is called, saith the Lord, who doeth all these things.

91. They said to him: Tell us who you are, so that we may believe in you. He said to them: You examine the face of the sky and of the earth, yet you do not recognize Him who is here with you, and you do not know how to seek in (to inquire of Him at) this moment (you do not know how to take advantage of this opportunity).

We have lived with, are acquainted with and know the signs of the physical world. We can tell if it is going to rain or what kind of plant is growing in a place, but we are not familiar with the spiritual world, even enough to tell that the messiah is walking among us.

John 9:36 He answered, And who is he, sir? Tell me, so that I may believe in him.

Luke 12:54-56 He also said to the crowds, When you see a cloud rising in the west, you immediately say, It is going to rain; and so it happens. And when you see the south wind blowing, you say, There will be scorching heat; and it happens. You hypocrites! You know how to interpret the appearance of earth and sky, but why do you not know how to interpret the present time?

92. Jesus said: Seek and you will find. But in the past I did not answer the questions you asked. Now I wish to tell them to you, but you do not ask about (no longer seek) them.

John 16:1 These things have I spoken unto you, that ye should not be offended.

2 They shall put you out of the synagogues: yea, the time cometh, that whosoever killeth you will think that he doeth God service.

3 And these things will they do unto you, because they have not known the Father, nor me.

4 But these things have I told you, that when the time shall come, ye may remember that I told you of them. And these things I said not unto you at the beginning, because I was with you.

5 But now I go my way to him that sent me; and none of you asketh me, Whither goest thou?

Matthew 7:7 Ask, and it will be given you; search, and you will find; knock, and the door will be opened for you.

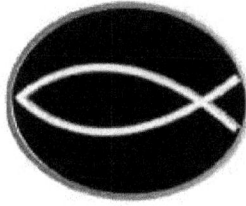

93. Jesus said: Do not give what is sacred to the dogs, lest they throw it on the dung heap. Do not cast the pearls to the swine, lest they cause it to become dung (mud).

This passage has been said by various scholars to refer to intercourse, Eucharist, or knowledge. This is a "Gnostic" gospel, after all, so we will assume he is referring to the secret and holy knowledge. The Gnosis.

Matthew 7:6 Do not give what is holy to dogs; and do not throw your pearls before swine, or they will trample them under foot and turn and maul you.

94. Jesus said: Whoever seeks will find. And whoever knocks, it will be opened to him.

When this passage appears in the Bible, some authors are quick to point out that the verb tense indicates a continuing action. That is, continue to knock and continue to seek, Do not stop knocking and seeking. A casual attempt will not get you where you need to go.

Matthew 7:8 For everyone who asks receives, and everyone who searches finds, and for everyone who knocks, the door will be opened.

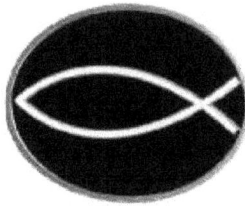

95. Jesus said: If you have money, do not lend at interest, but rather give it to those from whom you will not be repaid.

Do not give with the though to what you will get back. Give freely, out of compassion, not greed or expectation.

Luke 6:34-35 If you lend to those from whom you hope to receive, what credit is that to you? Even sinners lend to sinners, to receive as much again. But love your enemies, do good, and lend, expecting nothing in return. Your reward will be great, and you will be children of the Most High; for he is kind to the ungrateful and the wicked.

96. Jesus said: The Kingdom of the Father is like a woman who has taken a little yeast and hidden it in dough. She produced large loaves of it. Whoever has ears, let him hear!

Gnosis will be hidden in the world, scattered among the seekers, but when it breaks forth it will have spread and will be a notable force. This parable is like that of the tiny mustard seed growing into a large tree.

Matthew 13:33 He told them another parable: The kingdom of heaven is like yeast that a woman took and mixed in with three measures of flour until all of it was leavened.

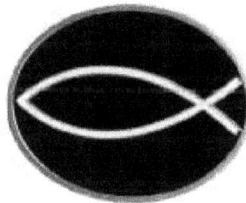

97. Jesus said: The Kingdom of the Father is like a woman who was carrying a jar full of grain (meal or flour). While she was walking on a road far from home, the handle of the jar broke and the grain poured out behind her onto the road. She did not know it. She had noticed no problem. When she arrived in her house, she set the jar down and found it empty.

Many times men stumble over the truth and then, after picking themselves up, they walk away as if nothing has happened. One of the dangers of epiphanies is that they are powerful at the time but if you do not nurture them they will fade away little by little and be lost.

98. Jesus said: The Kingdom of the Father is like someone who wished to slay a prominent person. While still in his own house he drew his sword and thrust it into the wall in order to test whether his hand would be strong enough. Then he went and slew the prominent person.

There are two messages here. Firstly – Count the cost and test your strength and tenacity before you begin. Half measures leave you worse off than before. Secondly – The strong man you are slaying is you. Your ego, your ignorance, and your splintered self; the you that you know will not endure.

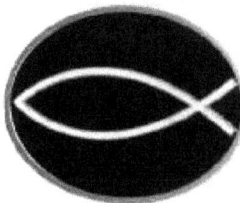

99. His Disciples said to him: Your brethren and your mother are standing outside. He said to them: Those here who do my Father's desires are my Brethren and my Mother. It is they who will enter the Kingdom of my Father.

The operative phrase here is "the kingdom of MY FATHER". Those who are connected to the Father and part of his family are siblings. None other can make the claim. The heavenly family trumps the corporeal familial connections. Seldom are members of the same family born under the same roof. Family is gathered along the way.

Matthew 12:46-50 While he was still speaking to the crowds, his mother and his brothers were standing outside, wanting to speak to him. Someone told him, Look, your mother and your brothers are standing outside, wanting to speak to you. But to the one who had told him this, Jesus replied, Who is my mother, and who are my brothers? And pointing to his disciples, he said, Here are my mother and my brothers! For whoever does the will of my Father in heaven is my brother and sister and mother.

100. They showed Jesus a gold coin, and said to him: The agents of Caesar extort taxes from us. He said to them: Give

the things of Caesar to Caesar, give the things of God to God, and give to me what is mine.

R. McL. Wilson writes: "Grant and Freedman rightly note that Thomas does not speak of the kingdom *of God*, and that indeed 'God' is mentioned only once (logion 100), and there evidently as subordinate to Jesus. Their inference that Thomas may be reserving the name 'God' for use as that of an inferior power is also probably correct, and serves to confirm the Gnostic character of the book; as already noted, the God of the Old Testament is in the Gnostic systems degraded to the status of creator and ruler of this present evil world." (*Studies in the Gospel of Thomas*, p. 27)

It is the Demiurge that created this world. He fights to keep all souls enslaved to him in worship and obedience. Caesar and the Demiurge are both tyrants. Give them what is owed them but Jesus demands those that are his.

Mark 12:14-17 Is it lawful to pay taxes to the emperor, or not? Should we pay them, or should we not? But knowing their hypocrisy, he said to them, Why are you putting me to the test? Bring me a denarius and let me see it. And they brought one. Then he said to them, Whose head is this, and whose title? They answered, The emperor's. Jesus said to them, Give to the emperor the things that are the emperor's, and to God the things that are God's. And they were utterly amazed at him.

101. Jesus said: Whoever does not hate his father and his mother, as I do, will not be able to become my Disciple. And whoever does not love his father and his mother, as I do, will not be able to become my disciple. For my mother bore me, yet my true Mother gave me the life.

Here, we again see the divergent views of earthly family ties and heavenly family ties. In this case the mother is the Holy Spirit, which in Hebrew is a feminine word and entity that gives spiritual life.

Matthew 10:37 Whoever loves father or mother more than me is not worthy of me; and whoever loves son or daughter more than me is not worthy of me.

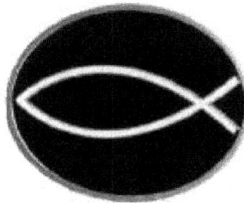

102. Jesus said: Damn these Pharisees. They are like a dog sleeping in the feed trough of oxen. For neither does he eat, nor does he allow the oxen to eat.

The learned teachers had all the information at hand to understand the kingdom, but they held to tradition and law and forced others to do the same, refusing to let them come to the knowledge of the truth.

J. D. Crossan writes: "The 'dog in the manger' is apparently a Greek proverb going back to 'very ancient times' (Moravcsik: 85). (1) It is included among the Greek proverbs attributed to Aesop: 'a dog lying in the manger who does not eat himself but hinders the donkey from doing so'

Matthew 2:13 But woe unto you, scribes and Pharisees, hypocrites! because you shut the kingdom of heaven against men; for you neither enter yourselves, nor allow those who would enter to go in.

103. Jesus said: Blessed (happy) is the person who knows at what place of the house the bandits may break in, so that he can rise and collect his things and prepare himself before they enter.

This parable or saying looks like #21, but instead of addressing the time of an attack, this one addresses the place. Still, watch, keep vigilant, and be prepared.

Matthew 24:43 But understand this: if the owner of the house had known in what part of the night the thief was coming, he would have stayed awake and would not have let his house be broken into.

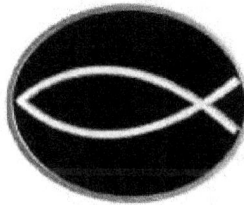

104. They said to him: Come, let us pray today and let us fast. Jesus said: What sin have I committed? How have I been overcome (undone)? When the Bridegroom comes forth from the bridal chamber, then let them fast and let them pray.

Jesus is telling them that these external trapping of religion make no difference and they do not reflect the state of the person. A person who has committed no sin has no need of prayer and fasting.

105. Jesus said: Whoever acknowledges (comes to know) father and mother, will be called the son of a whore.

The established religious leaders often called Jesus a bastard, referring to the fact that there were claims he was not Joseph's child. Indeed, strictly speaking, on the mundane physical level, this is true. God, not Joseph, whom Mary is married to under Jewish law, is the father. Jesus knows his heavenly father and mother and knows from where he came.

In Against Celsus 1.28; 32 Origen cites the tradition that Jesus was the illegitimate child of Mary, who 'bore a child from a certain soldier named Panthera.' It is known from a gravestone that a Sidonian archer named Tiberius Julius Abdes Pantera was in fact stationed in Palestine around the time of the birth of Jesus.

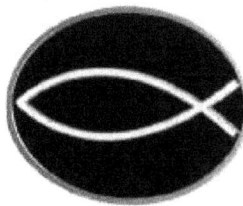

106. Jesus said: When you make the two one, you will become Sons of Man (children of Adam), and when you say to the mountain: Move! It will move.

Once again we have the theme of unity. The inner and outer, the male and female, and the higher and lower parts of a person must be brought into unity so that when one sets oneself to a task there is not a single part of the person arguing against the envisioned goal. It is not faith that moves the mountain. It is the unity of the person. Nowhere in this saying is faith mentioned.

It should be abundantly clear by now that the Gospel of Thomas is in fact a book of mystical unity. This is its theme and purpose. (See saying 48.)

Mark 11:23 Truly I tell you, if you say to this mountain, Be taken up and thrown into the sea, and if you do not doubt in your heart, but believe that what you say will come to pass, it will be done for you.

107. Jesus said: The Kingdom is like a shepherd who has a

hundred sheep. The largest one of them went astray. He left the ninety-nine and sought for the one until he found it. Having searched until he was weary, he said to that sheep: I desire you more than the ninety-nine.

Like the big fish in saying 8 and the best pearl of saying 76, this sheep is the largest. Although this motif seems to defy the synoptic gospels, as they explain the father does not wish for even the smallest to perish (Matt 18:14 'So it is not the will of my father who is in heaven that one of these little ones should perish') we have a pattern that would suggest that the largest, greatest, fattest, best... are features that suggest the containment of gnosis. Let the things go, but seek and keep that which gives or contains gnosis.

Matthew 18:12-13 What do you think? If a shepherd has a hundred sheep, and one of them has gone astray, does he not leave the ninety-nine on the mountains and go in search of the one that went astray? And if he finds it, truly I tell you, he rejoices over it more than over the ninety-nine that never went astray.

108. Jesus said: Whoever drinks from my mouth will become

like me. I will become him, and the secrets will be revealed to him.

The mouth of the master feeds the soul. The mouth is the gateway to the soul, thus the words of his mouth is a soul-to-soul communication. Knowledge is imparted from the mouth and so it follows that for the Gnostics salvation comes from the mouth as the transmission of gnosis. In many mystery religions there are ritual where the priest breathes into the mouth of the initiate as a symbol of the passing of the mystery from one to the other. Jesus breathed on his disciples and said, "receive ye the Holy Ghost (Spirit). Ghost, breath, wind, and spirit are the same Greek word. So it was for the initiation of the Knights Templar whose master breathed on them as part of the initiation. Jesus is the breath and spirit of God. He is the water of life, the living water, the well, the ever-flowing river. Drink deeply.

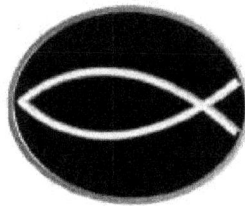

109. Jesus said: The Kingdom is like a person who had a treasure hidden in his field and knew nothing of it. After he died, he bequeathed it to his son. The son accepted the field knowing nothing of the treasure. He sold it. Then the person who bought it came and plowed it. He found the treasure. He began to lend money at interest to whomever he wished.

There is truth hidden everywhere and in everything, a piece of split wood and under a stone, as another saying explains. Yet, we give it away. We pass by, we sell our treasure because we are too slothful to dig. The point is almost lost in this saying that the field was obviously not used. It lay fallow. If the son had plowed the field he would have found the treasure.

Matthew 13:44 The kingdom of heaven is like treasure hidden in a field, which someone found and hid; then in his joy he goes and sells all that he has and buys that field.

110. Jesus said: Whoever has found the world (system) and becomes wealthy (enriched by it), let him renounce the world (system).

As is stated in saying 27, we should not depend on the world or society to define us or give us our worth. Our values or self-image should not come from the world. Renounce, walk away, untangle, and be free.

Mark 10:21-23 Then Jesus beholding him loved him, and said unto him, One thing thou lackest: go thy way, sell whatsoever thou hast, and give to the poor, and thou shalt have treasure in heaven: and come, take up the cross, and follow me. And he was sad at that saying, and went away grieved: for he had great possessions. And Jesus looked round about, and saith unto his disciples, How hardly shall they that have riches enter into the kingdom of God!

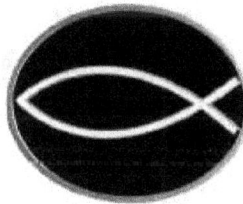

111. Jesus said: Heaven and earth will roll up (collapse and disappear) before you, but he who lives within the Living-One will neither see nor fear death. For, Jesus said: Whoever finds himself, of him the world is not worthy.

Another way of reading the verse may be:
Heaven and earth will open before you and the living will come forth out of the Living One and he will not see death or

fear (will not fear death) for, Jesus said: He who finds himself (keeps himself) the world is not worthy.

It is possible a later editor added the last part of this saying as an explanation. Still, we must find our place in the living God and the way to do that is to "find ourselves and keep ourselves from the dividing power of the world, which pulls us in so many directions. Be one and be here now – in the present with unity. In doing this we will emerge from the Living One fully alive.

112. Jesus said: Damned is the flesh which depends upon the soul. Damned is the soul which depends upon the flesh.

In the ancient concept, soul and spirit are not the same. Soul is the mental – emotional makeup of a being. Spirit is the life force from God. Here we are told that if the mental – emotional state depends on what the flesh is going through we are lost. There is a state beyond faith. It is knowing (Gnosis) and this will not be swayed by circumstances of the flesh. If the flesh depends on the soul it will perish as the soul steps out of it into freedom from the world. If the soul depends on the flesh it will be lost in cravings and disunity.

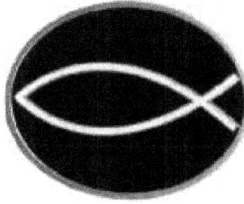

113. His Disciples said to him: When will the Kingdom come? Jesus said: It will not come by expectation (because you watch or wait for it). They will not say: Look here! or: Look there! But the Kingdom of the Father is spread upon the earth, and people do not realize it.

In saying 3 we are told not to believe those who say the kingdom is above or below you but it is inside you and outside you. It is everywhere if one were to see it. We can look to the Gospel of Mary 8,11-22 for comparison: "When the blessed one had said these things, he greeted them all, saying, 'Peace be with you. Acquire my peace for yourselves. Watch that no one mislead you, saying, "Look, here," or "Look, there," for the child of humankind is within you. Follow him. Those who seek him will find him. Go, then, and preach the gospel of the kingdom.'" (*The Gospel of Thomas: The Hidden Sayings of Jesus*, p. 108)

Luke 17:20 And when he was demanded of by the Pharisees, when the kingdom of God should come, he answered them and said, The kingdom of God cometh not with observation: Neither shall they say, Lo-Here! Lo-There! For, behold, the kingdom of God is within you.

(Saying 114 was written later and was added to the original text.)

114. Simon Peter said to them: Send Mary away from us, for women are not worthy of this life. Jesus said: See, I will draw her into me so that I make her male, in order that she herself will become a living spirit like you males. For every female who becomes male will enter the Kingdom of the Heavens.

Even though we are told there is no gender in heaven, no marriage, no differences in spirit between male and female, all angels are male. This is a metaphor from the time indicating a high (male) and lower (female) state. It is a statement using social values. We are told to cast off our garments of this body and become spiritual beings. Separate ourselves from the world. Shake off this mortal coil. Become higher creatures.

Summation

Having read the words of Thomas, what can we now say? Are these the words of Jesus? Is this a true catalog of the sayings, insights, and wisdom of the living Christ? Is Thomas simply conveying to us his memories of what he heard from Jesus when he walked the earth and taught the people? If these sayings are true they force us to reexamine modern, orthodox Christianity. Moreover, they force us to examine ourselves.

In the words of Jesus we find a plea, a command, to reach inside and reveal our true self. In discovering and knowing ourselves on the deepest level we will understand the Kingdom of Heaven, the Gnosis, is within us – it has always been. Upon realizing this truth we will know ourselves for what we are; the sons and daughters of the living God.

Jesus warns against organized religion. He steers us away from priests who steal the keys of the kingdom, keeping the truth from the people. Heaven is not above us, nor below us, nor in the hands of others, and not in any institution. God is in you and around you and there heaven must be also. He adds that we cannot do this alone. We need God's grace to draw us and make us realize we want and need more. It is up to God to make us homesick for the Kingdom.

It is no wonder that the Gospel of Thomas was suppressed by the early church. As the church struggled to consolidate its authority and power, the enemy would have been individual, spiritual advancement independent of ritual and rule. Yet, that is the essence of what the Protestant church calls salvation, if all other rituals and man-made rules were abandoned. It is the awakening caused by a personal encounter with truth itself – God, and when you are awake, fully awake, you can never fall asleep to the truth again. But the church has fallen asleep again and again, from reformation to reformation. Always, the body politic of the church struggles to suppress or even kill those rebels that have in some way awakened to the truth.

If you have ever felt as if there was more to existence than you could see, that there was another world just behind the curtain of your mind, that was just out of reach, which contained the full truth the words of Jesus will echo within you and lead you into light.

What is the essential wisdom within The Gospel of Thomas? Simply this; the search for self is the most difficult and troubling journey anyone could ever attempt, but it is also the only path with lasting spiritual results. If you can find what is real and honest within you, and if you have the courage to bring it forth, you will gain peace and strength and freedom forever. To deny your selfishness is to refuse to overcome it. To deny your blindness is to be held hostage by it. To ignore the longing in your heart for God is to die without knowing Him. Worst of all, to refuse to bring forth the true and holy part of you is to be destroyed by it as it sours and turns rancid within you, unborn and unseen. In this state we are neither true to God nor ourselves. We are lost and destined to suffer.

If we understand the Gospel we understand the clear and elegant truth. God is in us and outside of us, impossible to miss, undeniable to those who seek, and irresistible in His grace. He is the forgiving and loving father who awaits our return. A child knows the way and old men may realize they have lost the way, but the masses become so involved in the "world system" the way to God is forgotten or ignored.

"What must we do to be saved?" has been the same question posed for thousands of years. Jesus' answer in The Gospel of Thomas is shockingly simple. "Become passers by" and " bring forth what is within you". What does this mean? Become detached. Don't allow the world to posses you, but instead view it as though you are watching from a distance, and walking through a field. Separate yourself from feelings based in a world that is temporary and meaningless. Instead, focus on what is real within you. Find that part of you that is part of Him. Keep it, let it gestate, and give birth to it in your words, deeds, and thoughts. Reject all else.

How will you know it is done? What is the sign of your father in you? It is peace in the midst of motion. It is movement and rest. Whether the motion is external chaos or it is the emotions of anger or fear, there is peace and rest in your spirit. As Jesus commanded the storm, "peace, be still", He also commands us when he says, "Peace, peace I give to you. My peace I give to you, not as the world gives it, but as I alone can give it". But first, we must understand and obey.

Whoever finds the interpretation of these sayings will not taste death.

Let he who seeks not stop seeking until he finds, and when he finds he will be troubled, and when he has been troubled he will marvel (be astonished) and he will reign over all and in reigning, he will find rest.

If those who lead you say to you: Look, the Kingdom is in the sky, then the birds of the sky would enter before you. If they

say to you: It is in the sea, then the fish of the sea would enter ahead of you. But the Kingdom of God exists within you and it exists outside of you. Those who come to know (recognize) themselves will find it, and when you come to know yourselves you will become known and you will realize that you are the children of the Living Father. Yet if you do not come to know yourselves then you will dwell in poverty and it will be you who are that poverty.

Recognize what is in front of your face, and what has been hidden from you will be revealed to you. For there is nothing hidden which will not be revealed (become manifest), and nothing buried that will not be raised.

I will give to you what eye has not seen, what ear has not heard, what hand has not touched, and what has not occurred to the mind of man.

Unless you fast from the world (system), you will not find the Kingdom of God.

I stood in the midst of the world. In the flesh I appeared to them. I found them all drunk; I found none thirsty among them. My soul grieved for the sons of men, for they are blind in their hearts and do not see that they came into the world empty and they are destined (determined) to leave the world empty. However, now they are drunk. When they have shaken off their wine, then they will repent (change their ways).

Many times have you yearned to hear these sayings which I speak to you, and you have no one else from whom to hear them. There will be days when you will seek me but you will not find me.

Become passers-by.

Blessed is the solitary and chosen, for you will find the Kingdom. You have come from it, and unto it you will return. If they said to you: From where do you come? Say to them: We have come from the Light, the place where the Light came into existence of its own accord and he stood and appeared in their image. If they say to you: Is it you? (Who are you?), say: We are his Sons and we are the chosen of the Living Father. If they ask you: What is the sign of your Father in you? Say to them: It is movement with rest.

Those who know everything but themselves, lack everything. (whoever knows the all and still feels a personal lacking, he is completely deficient).

If you bring forth what is within you, it will save you. If you do not have it within you to bring forth, that which you lack will destroy you.

"I-Am" the Light who is over all things, "I-Am" the All. From me all came forth and to me all return (The All came from me and the All has come to me). Split wood, there am I. Lift up the stone and there you will find me.

Whoever is close to me is close to the fire, and whoever is far from me is far from the Kingdom.

Whoever drinks from my mouth will become like me. I will become him, and the secrets will be revealed to him.

Heaven and earth will roll up before you, but he who lives within the Living-One will neither see nor fear death. Whoever finds himself, of him the world is not worthy.

Bibliography

The Scholars' Translation of the Gospel of Thomas
by Stephen Patterson and Marvin Meyer

The Complete Gospels: Annotated Scholars Version.*
Copyright 1992, 1994 by Polebridge Press

The Other Gospels: Non-Canonical Texts. Philadelphia:
Westminster, 1982.

The New Testament and Other Early Christian Writings: A
Reader. New York: Oxford University Press, 1998.

The Apocryphal New Testament. Oxford: Clarendon, 1993.

The Gospel of Thomas: The Hidden Sayings of Jesus. San
Fransisco: HarperCollins, 1992.

Vol. 1 of New Testament Apocrypha. Westminster/John Knox,
1991.

Lectures of Stephen Hoeller through Gnosis.org

Nag Hammadi Library In English. San Fransisco: HarperCollins, 1988.

Nag Hammadi Codex II,2-7 Together With XIII,2*, BRIT. LIB. OR. 4926(1), and P.OXY. 1, 654, 655. Vol. 1. New York: Brill, 1989.

The Greek Fragments.Nag Hammadi Codex II,2-7
Edited by Bentley Layton. Vol. 1. New York: Brill, 1989.
Critical Greek Text.

The Oxyrhynchus Logoi of Jesus and the Coptic Gospel According to Thomas. London: Geoffrey Chapman, 1971.

The Sayings of Jesus From Oxyrhynchus. Cambridge: Cambridge University Press, 1920.

New Sayings of Jesus. The Oxyrhynchus Papyri. London: Egypt Exploration Fund, 1904.

Look for other fine books by Joseph Lumpkin.

For a complete catalog of books go to:
http://www.fifthestatepub.com

The Lost Book Of Enoch: A Comprehensive Transliteration,
ISBN: 0974633666

The Books of Enoch: A Complete Volume Containing 1 Enoch (The
Ethiopic Book of Enoch), 2 Enoch (The Slavonic Secrets of Enoch), 3
Enoch (The Hebrew Book of Enoch)
ISBN-13: 978-1933580807

The Encyclopedia of Lost and Rejected Scriptures: The
Pseudepigrapha and Apocrypha
ISBN-13: 978-1933580913

The Book of Jubilees; The Little Genesis, The Apocalypse of Moses
ISBN: 193358009

The Book Of Jasher
The J. H. Parry Text in Modern English
ISBN: 1933580143

The Gnostic Gospels of Philip, Mary Magdalene, and Thomas ISBN: 1933580135

The Gospel of Thomas: A Contemporary Translation
ISBN: 0976823349

Fallen Angels, The Watchers, and the Origins of Evil:
A Problem of Choice
ISBN: 1933580100

End of Days: The Apocalyptic Writings
The Apocalypse of Abraham, The Apocalypse of Thomas, or The Revelation of Thomas, 4 Ezra, also referred to as 2 Esdras or the Apocalypse of Ezra, 2 Baruch, also known as the Syriac. Apocalypse of Baruch
ISBN: 1-933580-38-0

For audio interviews by Joseph Lumpkin go to:

http://fifthestatepub.com/feinterviews/

For video interviews go to:

http://fifthestatepub.com/media/video/

Don't forget to watch all of the segments on Youtube, and other video caching sites.